Self-Management and Efficiency: Large Corporations in Yugoslavia

STEPHEN R. SACKS

London
GEORGE ALLEN AND UNWIN
Boston   Sydney

© Stephen R. Sacks, 1983.
This book is copyright under the Berne Convention. No reproduction without permission. All rights reserved.

George Allen & Unwin (Publishers) Ltd,
40 Museum Street, London WC1A 1LU, UK

George Allen & Unwin (Publishers) Ltd,
Park Lane, Hemel Hempstead, Herts HP2 4TE, UK

Allen & Unwin, Inc.,
9 Winchester Terrace, Winchester, Mass 01890, USA

George Allen & Unwin Australia Pty Ltd,
8 Napier Street, North Sydney, NSW 2060, Australia

First published in 1983

British Library Cataloguing in Publication Data

Sacks, Stephen R.
   Self-management and efficiency: large corporations in Yugoslavia.
1. Works councils—Yugoslavia   2. Industrial management—Yugoslavia
I. Title
658.3'152'09497   HD5660.Y8
ISBN 0-04-334008-3

Library of Congress Cataloging in Publication Data

Sacks, Stephen R.
   Self-management and efficiency.
Bibliography: p.
1. Industrial management—Yugoslavia—Employee participation.
2. Industrial organization—Yugoslavia.
3. Corporations—Yugoslavia.   I. Title.
HD5660.Y8S14 1983   658.3'152'09497   83-14999
ISBN 0-04-334008-3

Set in 10 on 11 pt Times by
D. P. Media Limited, Hitchin, Hertfordshire
and printed in Great Britain by Billing and Sons Ltd,
London and Worcester

Contents

		Page	
Foreword			v
Introduction			vii
Chapter 1	Divisionalization in Yugoslav Corporations		1
Chapter 2	Giant Corporations in Yugoslavia		22
Chapter 3	The Theory of Transfer Prices		47
Chapter 4	The Efficiency of Divisionalized Corporations		58
Chapter 5	Investment Decisions in the Divisionalized Firm		75
Chapter 6	Case Studies		100
Chapter 7	Divisionalization in Other Socialist Countries		128
Chapter 8	Summary		143
References			151
Index			158

Our self-management system is a mixture of totalitarianism and anarchy.

(A Yugoslav industrial expert;
quoted in *The Economist*,
11 August, 1979, p. 45)

Foreword

I have previously conjectured that both the standard industrial organization apparatus for characterizing market structure and the transaction cost approach to the study of economic organization have application to socialist as well as capitalist economies. Stephen Sacks demonstrates that these conjectures are correct and helps to unify research on industrial organization and comparative economic systems in the process.

The Yugoslav economy is an interesting amalgam of socialist and capitalist organizational principles. It is thus particularly fitting that Professor Sacks should select Yugoslavia for a pioneering study of this kind. He plainly believes, moreover, that similar studies can be performed in other mixed economies. Indeed, there are lessons to be learned here that apply to the full range of economic organization in advanced as well as developing economies.

The study of economic organization at the microanalytic level that Professor Sacks employs is of relatively recent origin. Although it is both primitive and in need of refinements, new applications and conceptual refinements have continued to appear. I am therefore optimistic that progressively more leverage will be realized by recent and future developments. This approach to the study of economic organization takes seriously Percy Bridgeman's reminder to social scientists that 'the principal problem in understanding the actions of men is to understand how they think – how their minds work'. Self-conscious attention to the behavioral assumptions – of which bounded rationality and opportunism are among the more important — is clearly required.

Refutable implications of this approach are derived by identifying the critical dimensions with respect to which transactions differ and by assigning transactions to organizational structures (firms, divisions, markets, mixed modes) in a discriminating (mainly transaction cost economizing) way. The degree to which transactions are supported by specialized investments – transaction-specific physical or human capital – turns out to be critical in this connection. The same transaction cost reasoning that has been applied to the study of vertical integration, regulation and non-standard contracting in Western economies carries over to Yugoslav self-management, as Sacks' treatment of the latter convincingly demonstrates.

Both economists and organization theory specialists who are persuaded (or are prepared to contemplate the possibility) that firms are more than production functions to which an appropriate objective function is ascribed, but believe instead that internal organization matters, will find that their understanding of economic organization is deepened and extended by this book.

Oliver E. Williamson

To my wife, Christy, whose support made this book possible, and to Gordon and Jacob, who had to give up so much of their dad's time for The Book.

Introduction

Yugoslavia is widely viewed as a laboratory where experiments are conducted in market socialism and worker self-management. As with other laboratories, the results of the experiments done there have significance beyond its own boundaries. Especially now that the system has outlived Tito, observers believe that it can endure. Among the socialist countries, the results of these experiments are important to nations as diverse as Hungary, Poland, China and the Soviet Union. Hungary has gone furthest in establishing a partial market mechanism; Poland is struggling to find a better economic system; China is sending teams of observers to Belgrade; and in March of 1983 Soviet Party Secretary Andropov, who had supported early Hungarian innovations, said that 'the Soviet Union should learn from economic reforms in other socialist countries'. These and other countries are watching closely, not only the overall economic performance of Yugoslavia, but especially the details of enterprise structure. For many of these countries the success or failure of Yugoslavia's effort to break up large corporations into autonomous self-managed divisions will influence their own decisions regarding the economic system they adopt. They are more likely to adopt a system of worker self-management if it appears to be consistent with efficient large-scale production. And even without self-management, the socialist countries have much to learn about organizational structure from the Yugoslav system.

In western countries, too, there is interest in the outcome of Yugoslav experiments: worker participation in decision-making has become a political issue in Sweden, Belgium, the United Kingdom and France, among others; and certainly in West Germany, with its system of co-determination, there is interest. Even in the United States, where more than 5,000 enterprises are worker-owned, the viability of large self-managed enterprises is important. In some of these countries, concern with the concentration of political and economic power motivates the interest in this topic. In others it is a more narrowly economic concern with efficiency. Referring to the impressive performance of the West German and Japanese economies, MacMillan and Farmer (1979, p. 279) say that 'the ability to combine effective coordination with decentralized ownership may be a most important factor in the success of these two economies'. There are obvious similarities between Japanese zaibatsu and large Yugoslav enterprises: both use the notion of a corporate 'family' to embrace a set of partially autonomous divisions which buy from and sell to one another. Indeed, the current interest in the Japanese economy has led General Motors and other big corporations in the United States to seek closer ties with their suppliers. The idea is that closer vertical relationships between independent suppliers and their customers can make a market system work better. Such collaboration is particularly important in situations where rapid technological change causes uncertainty. Markets need not necessarily consist of pure, arm's length relationships. Indeed, the central idea of this book is that markets can operate within enterprises.

During the past two decades a considerable amount of research has been done on Yugoslavia's economic system, the world's only market socialism. Much of that research has been macroeconomic, focusing on growth, unemployment and inflation. Some has been microeconomic, examining Yugoslavia's labor-managed enterprises from both theoretical and empirical points of view. However, one of the most significant characteristics of the Yugoslav system has received little attention. This book is intended to fill an important gap in our understanding of that economy by examining a microeconomic topic that is the heart of the significance of the Yugoslav system, namely, the relationship among subdivisions within large labor-managed enterprises. Just as Yugoslavia has been a pioneer among socialist countries in using a price mechanism, instead of centralized planning, to coordinate the activities of separate enterprises, so too it has for nearly two decades been gradually reducing centralized decision-making *within* enterprises, and instead allowing increasingly autonomous subunits to negotiate internal transactions.

Thus, Yugoslavia's long-standing commitment to self-management by small work units has been extended during the past twenty years. Reforms, constitutional amendments and new economic laws have all contributed to the increasing independence of divisions within the firm. This raises a number of important questions. To what extent are the subunits of firms really autonomous? How do they relate to one another? How are transfer prices set and what effect do they have on production decisions and on economic efficiency? The problem of what price a sparkplug division should charge for the product that it provides to the engine division of the same firm has been studied in a capitalist framework, but until now this same question has not been considered in the context of a socialist labor-managed economy.

The central question to be answered by this book is whether the Yugoslavs' extensive implementation of their principle of self-management by small work units is costly in terms of economic efficiency. Are they atomizing their firms into inefficiently small fragments? Is the system of worker self-management appropriate only for small firms, perhaps handicrafts and agriculture? Can a modern industrial enterprise of efficient scale, indeed very large scale, be run that way? In order to answer these questions, this book applies to large Yugoslav firms the transactions cost analysis developed by Oliver Williamson. The logic of that approach allows us to view the Yugoslav corporation as a shell within which the cost of transactions is reduced because they are at least partially insulated from the opportunistic behavior that would be encountered outside the firm. The same analysis can be used to explain the creation of industrial associations in other socialist countries. There, too, an economic unit acts as a shell within which the activities of subunits are coordinated without interference from outside. Although I do not explicitly discuss Japanese zaibatsu, the Spanish cooperatives at Mondragon or General Motors and its suppliers, I believe that useful parallels can be drawn between those organizations and the Yugoslav firm.

It should be clear that this book does not provide a general introduction to the Yugoslav economy. Rather, it examines a particular topic that I believe to be very important. It is appropriate here to quote John Kenneth Galbraith's response to Robert Solow's accusation that, in *The New Industrial State*, Galbraith equates all economic activity with large firms: large corporations, he says, 'are not the whole of the economy. The remaining part of the economic system is not insignificant. It is not, however, the part of the economy with which this book is concerned' (1967, p. 111). I, like Galbraith, am not claiming to describe an entire economic system, but rather one significant part. Further, I think that in Yugoslavia, more than in the US, large firms are inherently interesting because a substantial body of economic theory suggests that self-managed firms will be small. This raises the question of whether there is a fundamental conflict between large corporations and the principle of self-management by small groups. The Yugoslav solution to this conflict is divisionalization – the breaking up of big corporations into sets of autonomous subunits.

By a similar logic, I have refrained from delving into the literature on motivation, incentives and alienation in self-managed firms. I do not deny the importance or relevance of that literature, but it is not the subject of this book.

The book begins with a description of the internal structure of large Yugoslav enterprises. The main point of the first chapter is that in Yugoslavia divisionalization of firms is extensive and meaningful. Divisions have considerable autonomy and buy from and sell to one another at transfer prices that affect production decisions as well as the distribution of income.

Chapter 2 examines several reasons for believing that firm size is important to the operation of market socialism and then shows that many firms in Yugoslavia are in fact very large, both relative to other firms in that country and by international standards. It also presents data on division size and on changes in size distributions over the period 1969–81.

Chapter 3 takes a theoretical view of transfer prices, and shows that under certain circumstances they can correct an inefficient allocation of labor and materials among divisions within the self-managed firm.

Chapter 4 is the heart of the book. In it I use Oliver Williamson's transactions cost analysis to show that divisionalization can increase economic efficiency while strengthening self-management. That is, there need not necessarily be a trade-off in which output is sacrificed in order to maintain self-management for small groups. The enterprise constitutes a shell within which autonomous groups use market transactions (perhaps somewhat modified) to coordinate their activities.

Chapter 5, like chapter 3, is more theoretical. It examines investment decisions by divisionalized labor-managed firms and thus sets the stage for chapter 6, which presents a number of case studies. These cases provide a detailed look at the internal workings of large Yugoslav enterprises, focusing especially on investment decisions and on the relationships among divisions regarding income distribution and transfer prices.

In chapter 7, I argue that the analysis of divisionalization within Yugoslav firms can also be used to understand the development, over the past twenty years, of industrial associations in many other socialist countries. Those countries are experimenting with changes in the size of their basic economic units and with their administrative organizational structure. The associations were created in an effort to balance costs of decision-making within economic units against the costs of decision-making outside those units. Thus they can be understood with the same concepts that I have used to examine Yugoslav firms.

Chapter 8 is a summary of the entire book.

I should like to express my gratitude to The National Academy of Sciences in Washington and to the Yugoslav Council of Academies of Sciences whose exchange agreement provided not only the funds but the official sanction that made an extended visit to Yugoslavia successful. I also want to thank Jadranko Bendeković, Dragomir Vojnić, Dražen Kalogjera, Dubravka Kunštek, and others at the Ekonomski Institut in Zagreb for their help. The National Council for Soviet and East European Research provided funds that freed my time for much of the writing of this book, and the Institute of International Studies at Berkeley kindly provided office space where I could work without interruption during a sabbatic year. I am very grateful to both organizations. Dr Savo Cvetanovski at the Yugoslav Press and Cultural Center in New York repeatedly supplied published statistics at times when I despaired of getting any response from the Yugoslav Federal Institute for Statistics. I am grateful also to Frank Stephen and Deborah Milenkovitch for their helpful comments on various parts of the manuscript.

Earlier versions of chapters 1 and 3 appeared in *The Journal of Comparative Economics* (Sacks, 1980; 1977) and some of the material in chapter 2 is taken from Sacks (1982).

Stephen R. Sacks
Storrs, Connecticut
March 1983

1 Divisionalization in Yugoslav Corporations

Introduction

For more than three decades the Yugoslav economy has been characterized by a continuing process of decentralization. The centralized command economy of 1945, patterned on the Soviet model, had by the early 1950s begun to develop into a system of self-management by independent enterprises. By 1965 the independence of enterprises from central-government control was fairly complete and a principle of autonomy for divisions *within* the enterprise had begun to evolve. These developments are a logical consequence of the fundamental principle that underlies the philosophy of the entire Yugoslav economic system: wherever possible small work units are to be organized as separate, independent entities.

From an economist's point of view, the desirability of divisionalizing enterprises is arguable: the issue has generated a substantial body of literature (largely in business-oriented journals) that deals with the merits of divisionalization in a capitalist environment.[1] Proponents cite various cases that support their position. For example, it is widely believed that General Motors saved itself from bankruptcy by dividing into autonomous divisions and that Ford Motor Company nearly failed because for a long time it did not do so. On the other hand, some large American firms (e.g. Republic Steel) prefer to operate without divisionalization. The same issue is significant in a socialist environment but has received little attention in western literature. In contemporary Yugoslavia the question of whether activities within the firm should be coordinated by an administrative or a market mechanism is of primary importance.

There are a number of questions one might ask about an economic system in which large corporations are run as though they were sets of smaller firms. Some particularly important questions concern transfer prices, that is, the prices at which intermediate goods and services are sold between divisions within a large firm. But these are only part of a larger question, namely, whether the Yugoslavs' extensive implementation of their principle of self-management by small work units will be costly in terms of economic efficiency. It is not easy to see whether

Yugoslavia is improving the efficiency of its system of resource allocation or atomizing its firms into inefficiently small fragments.

The purpose of this chapter is to describe the divisionalization of large socialist enterprises in Yugoslavia and to examine the autonomy of, and the relationship among, the divisions. While a number of fundamental analytical questions will be raised, the major purpose is not to evaluate these important developments, but rather to set the stage for the analysis of their economic significance which will be undertaken in the following chapters.

This chapter focuses first on the autonomy of the divisions of the Yugoslav enterprise, and then examines the transfer prices at which goods and services are sold between divisions. In the final section attention centers on the structure of the entity formed by a collection of divisions (an entity still regarded by Yugoslavs as an 'enterprise', although that word is no longer fasionable) and examines the ties that hold it together.

Autonomy of the basic organization of associated labor

For a long time special attention has been paid in Yugoslavia to the subunits of the enterprise.[2] As early as 1953 a subunit could be granted the status of legal person with the right to enter into contracts outside the enterprise. Further, the law stated that every unit able to perform its economic activity independently had the right to become an independent enterprise, although it needed permission from the rest of the enterprise to withdraw. Regulations issued in 1954 required that when a new plant was registered a statement had to be submitted specifying whether or not the new unit could act in its own name and in the name of the enterprise, whether or not the enterprise was liable for the subunit's debts, and whether or not it had a separate legal identity and bank account. If built at a separate location it had to have its own management organs, bookkeeping and bank account. A 1965 law strengthened the autonomy of enterprise subunits, and constitutional amendments in 1968 introduced new terminology that emphasizes the importance and independence of the subunits. These changes made explicit the possibility (already contained in earlier laws) that subunits may have the status of legal persons if their work is such that they can independently enter the marketplace.

In more recent years the importance of subunits has increased further. Constitutional amendments in 1971 (later embodied in the Constitution of 1974) increased their independence, and the Law on Associated Labor (LAL) of 1976 further strengthened this trend. According to current Yugoslav law, the basic economic unit is not the enterprise but the 'basic organization of associated labor', or BOAL, as the divisions are referred to in western literature. They are the holders of all social sector assets and have final authority in all decision-making. They may voluntarily join together to form enterprises,[3] but the extent to which they may delegate authority to central organs of the enterprise is limited. Major decisions that affect all divisions must be voted on by all of them. Perhaps most important for this study, every division has the right to buy or sell outside the enterprise.

Technically, income is earned solely by divisions, not by enterprises (LAL, articles 14 and 18). A division may earn income by (1) selling goods or services on domestic and foreign markets, (2) selling goods or services to other divisions within the enterprise, or (3) engaging in joint efforts with other divisions (so-called 'pooling of labor and resources'). Even income that is earned jointly with other divisions must be distributed in its entirety among the participating divisions; none may be considered 'enterprise income' (LAL, articles 70 and 82). Such distribution is to be made 'according to the contribution' of each division to the value of joint output (LAL, articles 66 and 82). In most cases this is done with transfer prices, but any objective measurement is allowed. The important point here is that each worker's income comes from his division, not directly from the enterprise.

Current law makes clear (LAL, articles 338–41) that every division has the right to separate off from its enterprise. The only restrictions are that it must give adequate notice and that it is responsible for fulfilling any obligations to which it had committed itself. This includes not only delivering goods promised to other divisions of the firm, but also compensating them in case the withdrawal would 'substantially diminish the income earning possibilities' of the remaining divisions. Such occurrences are rare but there are some examples. For instance, a division of Radio Industrija Zagreb (RIZ) left to become part of another electronics enterprise that had a product line more appropriate to that division's activities; Agrocommerce of Titograd separated from Agrooprema of Belgrade and they became competitors; workers at Alumina in Skopje voted to pull out of Energoinvest of Sarajevo after a dispute over investment in duplicate capacity.[4]

The legal definition of a division is not easy to implement. The law states that if the performance of a subunit of an enterprise 'can be expressed in terms of value within the work organization or on the market . . . the workers . . . shall have the right and duty to organize . . . [that unit] as a basic organization of associated labor'.[5] Furthermore, a division must have only one activity and cannot perform related activities if it is possible to organize a separate division for those other activities. These principles are so imprecise that there is considerable debate and disagreement among Yugoslav businessmen, economists and lawyers over how to meet legal and practical requirements of the law. The problems that can arise are illustrated by a discussion I heard at a conference of business lawyers in Zagreb. The topic was whether selling alcoholic and non-alcoholic drinks constitute separate activities; if so, it would seem that a café must have two divisions, even though the same employees work in both. This is, of course, an extreme example, but it illustrates the kind of problem the new rules have raised.

In practice, a café with a dozen employees will not have more than one division. However, a chain of cafés with a dozen workers in each may or may not be organized with each establishment as a separate division. There is no general rule in such matters. In Montenegro in a chain of fifty-two hotels there was considerable debate over whether to have fifty-two divisions or a smaller number. In the end they agreed to group hotels on a geographical basis into eighteen divisions. Similarly, a manufacturer of eyeglass frames and lenses had its 110 retail shops organized into sixteen divisions. Some of these divisions included all of their shops in a republic and others included only those in a single city. The central management of the enterprise argued for consolidation of all 110 shops into a single division. Their reason, although not publicly admitted, was that they wanted to reduce and make more enforceable the firm's agreed limit (then 30 per cent) on the shops' sales of goods made by other manufacturers.

In manufacturing enterprises a single division often includes all workers involved in a particular product line from raw material to finished product. For example, in a Zagreb firm, workers who melt cocoa, make a particular style of hard chocolate and package it are all in one division. Those who work on a different type of candy are in a separate division, although some of the boxes sold by this firm in retail stores contain candy from several different divisions. In another firm the three vertical steps (melting, forming the candy and packaging) might be organized into three separate divisions. Similarly, in one firm all the steps in producing a particular shoe are included in one division, while in another firm the uppers and soles are sold by two divisions to a third division that then sews them together. A Slovenian electronics firm with 27,000 workers is divided into sixty-six divisions. Most correspond to a particular product (e.g. broadcast antennae, motors for home appliances, telephone switchboards, etc.), but some are defined on functional lines (e.g. data processing center, engineering design, equipment installation and repair, workers' restaurant, etc.).

In most enterprises certain administrative services that are provided to all of the divisions of an enterprise are performed not by divisions but by 'work communities'. The law specifies that planning, personnel services, bookkeeping, legal services, maintenance and security of buildings, filing and typing are to be organized in this way. Another group of activities may be viewed either as providing administrative services to other divisions or as directly creating something of measurable value, and hence can be organized either as work communities or as divisions. These include marketing, project design, engineering and R & D, data processing and personnel training (LAL, articles 400–7; see also Constitution, articles 29 and 30). Work communities operate under special restrictions. They may not withdraw from the enterprise and they can be dissolved at the discretion of the divisions, which would then divide up any assets. They have no funds of their own: by mutual agreement the divisions provide money to pay their costs, including personal and collective consumption for the workers at a rate equal to the average earned in the divisions. When permitted, organizing such activities as a division rather than a work community allows somewhat greater flexibility. Withdrawal from the enterprise still requires permission of the other divisions, but it is allowed to sell services outside the enterprise. For example, a Montenegrin hotel enterprise changed the status of its purchasing department from that of work community to that of division so that it could supply food to an off-shore oil rig.

In order to get some sense of the actual size of divisions, I have calculated averages for a sample of sixty-seven large industrial enterprises in 1978. The size of these enterprises varied from 1,519 to 37,512 workers, the average size being 12,461. The number of divisions per enterprise varied from 6 to 180 and averaged 47 divisions. Average division size can be calculated in two ways: the total number of workers in all sixty-seven enterprises can be divided by the total number of divisions; or the average division size can be calculated for each enterprise and then these averages can be averaged. Although the data do not suggest that larger enterprises have larger divisions, it still seems wise to avoid giving more weight to the larger enterprises, so I used the second method. Average division size varied from 88 to 766 workers, the unweighted average being 315 workers per division. For the same year, a sample of twenty-four large trade sector enterprises averaged 5,580 workers divided into an average of thirty-nine divisions. The average division size was 177 workers. Apparently, these trade sector firms employ about half as many workers as do the industrial enterprises and divide them into nearly as many divisions.

The most obvious advantage of dividing up these large enterprises is the improvement in incentives for hard work. The motivational value of a system based on profit sharing among workers is greater when several hundred rather than several thousand others share the results of any incremental effort by each worker (see Tyson, 1979). The same type of logic suggests that any collective decision to work harder (or even to maintain a previous level of effort) can be more effectively implemented in a smaller group; that is, mutual monitoring of co-workers' effort is easier. Along different lines, it is interesting to note that one finds in business journals a view of large enterprises that is analogous to a view of the Soviet-type economy found in comparative systems literature: the only way to make subunits act in the best interests of the whole is to give them considerable autonomy and to evaluate (and reward) them on the profit they earn. It should be noted that these observations do not apply to Yugoslav 'work communities'.

The extreme autonomy of the divisions (which is not merely a legal principle but in many cases a practical reality) is perhaps best demonstrated by an examination of transfer prices. But first a few words are needed concerning the more general role of competition and prices in the Yugoslav economy. Firms do not always compete with one another. Indeed, collusion and market sharing are common. But as Comisso (1980, p. 200) points out, the pressures to collude and divide up markets are often *political* pressures, which are applied by governments to offset the reluctance of firms and divisions to suppress the apparently strong tendency to compete. While 'excessive' competition is often interregional (in one republic a light bulb plant will be built or an airline established despite excess capacity in another republic), it can also be found within a single republic. For example, Comisso cites the efforts of the Serbian government to force manufacturers of household appliances to agree on complementary product lines. In this case the effort was to persuade producers of thirty-eight different products to specialize, at least with regard to air conditioners, electric motors, water heaters and space heaters (*Ekonomska Politika*, 16 May, 1977, p. 19). Similarly, in 1981 the provincial government in Kosovo tried to persuade its metal processing industry to achieve closer coordination among its eighteen work organizations, fourteen divisions and one complex enterprise (*Bulletin*, 23 June, 1981, p. 3). In both these cases the problem of overcapacity resulted from each producer's determination to go ahead and build production facilities that would allow it to compete in all product lines. In a peculiar reversal of the traditional problem in the United States, the Yugoslav situation seems, at least in some cases, to be one of competition persisting despite government efforts to suppress it.

Of course, this view should not be overstated, and in any case it applies more to competition between firms than to competition within firms. Indeed, perhaps the major difference between relationships between and within firms is the greater likelihood of successful collusion between divisions within the firm. On the other hand, even within the firm, prices play a very important role. Despite extensive discussion of 'polycentric planning', the fact is that the Yugoslav system of planning is simply too vague to be plausible as a mechanism for decision-making. The standard rhetoric is presented by Schrenk (1981, p. 3): 'Expectations and ambitions of individual BOALs and enterprises [are] iteratively reconciled for consistency'; 'Harmonized micro-plans have to be consistent . . . '; 'Creation of universal transparency . . . and the elimination of deviations from planned (preagreed) actions'; 'Calibration of investment through ex ante coordination. . . .' Such notions may serve to facilitate the operation of a market but cannot *replace* prices as the basis for production decisions. Referring to a plethora of self-management agreements, Comisso (1980, p. 200) says 'many existed only on paper, . . . while others were simply suspended . . .'. In the absence of any functional alternative mechanism, the Yugoslav system is essentially a set of contracts based on prices.

Transfer Prices

Transfer prices are the prices charged for goods and services sold between divisions within an enterprise. They are determined by intensive negotiations between buyer and seller, who are, in fact, bargaining over their own incomes, and who actually sign a legally binding contract specifying prices and quantities. These negotiations are not a sham: there have been a few cases where deliveries of goods between divisions in an enterprise were halted (briefly) because agreement on a transfer price had not been reached.[6]

An important question is whether or not production decisions are based on transfer prices. In some cases divisions seem to agree first on quantities and then on prices. That is, they might appear not to affect the allocation of resources but only the distribution of income. However, since there usually is a keen awareness of outside alternatives, every division has a pretty good idea of the transfer prices before output decisions are made and thus it is likely that they do affect production plans. At the very least, last year's prices are known, so one could argue that output decisions are based on lagged transfer prices. Further, if they are nothing but an income distribution device and do not determine production decisions, then we are left without an explanation of how such basic decisions are made.

Transfer prices are among the most important factors to be considered in assessing the impact of divisionalization of Yugoslav firms on the efficiency of resource allocation. Chapter 3 shows that decentralization within enterprises can lead to an inefficient allocation of labor within the firm, but that the use of transfer prices, if they are equal to external market prices, can correct this inefficiency.

While the relationship among the divisions in Yugoslav enterprises is not quite the pure market relationship that is sometimes claimed, in most enterprises intermediate goods and services are in fact sold at transfer prices that at least approximate market prices. It is the threat of buying or selling outside the enterprise that prevents much deviation. If the transfer price were much higher than the price on external markets, the division that uses the service or intermediate product, being free to buy outside the enterprise, would do so; if the transfer price were much lower, the seller would instead sell on outside markets. For example, in a Belgrade drug firm the transfer price for plastic containers was lowered after the antibiotic division began purchasing them from a Slovenian firm. The important point is that there is no central authority within the enterprise that can dictate transfer prices, nor can anyone force a settlement of a dispute. Of course, the enterprise central management is often effective in persuading divisions to reach an agreement.

In some cases transfer prices are quite explicitly tied to world prices. For example, according to an agreement made in 1977 (*Ekonomska Politika*, 17 October, 1977, pp. 22–3), the domestic prices of bauxite and primary alumina are the prices published in London in the *Metal Bulletin*. A system of six-month averages and proportional adjustments dampens the fluctuations of the domestic prices by partially insulating them from the volatility of world prices, and a procedure for evaluating the quality of the ore is needed to determine the exact price of a shipment of bauxite. But it seems clear that within a complex enterprise like Boris Kidrić Aluminum, which is integrated from mining through refining to fabrication, transfer prices are closely tied to external market prices.

In cases where a transfer price is not exactly equal to the corresponding external price, it often goes up when the external price rises and down when the external price falls. For instance, at the Sisak steel mill the transfer price for sheet steel sold to another division is pegged at 6 per cent below the price on European markets.

If there is no outside market, it is sometimes possible for a division to seek bids from outside firms. For example, a division of a Croatian shipyard requested bids from foundries for the fabrication of certain metal parts used in making welding machines; the shipyard's own foundry bid high and the job went to an outside foundry. In some cases the private sector can provide services whose prices serve as a benchmark for transfer prices within large enterprises (see Sacks, 1978). For example, in a large firm near Zagreb the transportation division charges the central office for car and driver at a rate equal to that charged by local private taxis. Similarly, in another firm the maintenance shop lowered its price for painting the name on company trucks to meet a price bid by a private sector painter.

In some cases the divisions in an enterprise create an adjustment mechanism such that transfer prices change with the price of a final product. For example, the twenty-nine divisions in a tractor enterprise in Belgrade agreed that all transfer prices would adjust in proportion to changes in the final price of their tractors (*Politika*, 13 February, 1977, p. 10). Thus, annual negotiations are essentially a matter of determining each division's percentage participation in total enterprise income. This is not in any essential way different from negotiating an absolute price, and in particular it allows the possibility that a division will react to a price change by altering its output (at the next round of contract talks). An effect of one price on others is, of course, a normal part of a market system, although in this case the effect on prices of inputs may not be exactly the same as if input prices were set in absolute terms. Normally, when the price of a final product changes, the effect on the price of an input depends on its cost as a proportion of total cost and on the availability of substitutes. The requirement of a proportional price adjustment may make the input price either higher or lower than it would otherwise be, but this rigidity is a short-run phenomenon. In the long run, under new contracts the input price will approach the same equilibrium it would have in the absence of this rigidity. But this income-sharing mechanism does mean that any change in market conditions will be transmitted more immediately from a final product to inputs related to it by derived demand, thus tending to strengthen the sense of enterprise solidarity.

Often the price on an external market is taken as a starting point for transfer-price negotiations, which then focus on the costs of the seller. From the point of view of overall efficiency, this is particularly desirable in cases where external markets are not perfectly competitive and hence transfer prices set equal to market prices would not accurately measure marginal cost. Both buyer and seller are required to make a complete disclosure of their costs and revenues, as well as of the incomes of its workers, so social pressure tends to push the transfer price to a level that yields a 'fair' distribution of profit. This may relieve the seller of competitive pressure to minimize its own costs; but often substantial pressure comes from the fact that the division buying the intermediate good must sell a final product on competitive domestic or world markets.

There are, of course, some situations in which transfer prices deviate substantially from market prices. There are a number of reasons for this. First, there are obvious explanations like the fact that the external price includes some part of transportation costs or the cost of packaging and shipping. In such cases we would expect a lower price when the buyer and seller are physically located together. Similarly, economies of scale in production, ease of billing, reduced likelihood of bad debts, etc. may explain a lower transfer price. Several of these explanations can be put under the heading of reduced uncertainty.

There are also other reasons why transfer prices in Yugoslav firms do not always equal external prices. Much of the explanation lies in the sense of solidarity with sister divisions with which long-term relationships have been established. In some instances social or political pressure causes one division to agree to a transfer price favorable to another so as to improve the financial health of the latter; thus the transfer price is hiding an intentional transfer of funds. But even in situations where a transfer price differs from an external price there is often a keen awareness of the market price. Thus, it is clear to decision-makers what they are 'paying' for enterprise solidarity.

In cases where one division has helped finance expansion or modernization of another, the transfer price is likely to be favorable to the lender. However, the law states that a price agreement may not last longer than the period of repayment of the investment funds, and in any case if workers in the other division think the price is unfair they can refuse the deal at the outset or else take the matter to court after the funds are invested (LAL, articles 85 and 86). (A court can declare a price unfair and order it changed.) Often the borrower agrees to buy or sell a specific quantity of some intermediate good at a price favorable to the lender and is free to seek better prices outside the enterprise for the remainder of its capacity.

The costs of 'work communities' that provide administrative services are in principle paid by only those divisions that use the services. Where it is possible to measure use of such services, divisions pay in proportion to the amount of service used; otherwise they pay in proportion to their size. In some firms, if a division asks for extra, unplanned services it has to pay for them separately.

In many cases the effect of transfer prices on the behavior of the enterprise is clearly beneficial. For instance, in a Zagreb drug firm it was the use of transfer prices that made clear the inefficiency of employing tailors to make laboratory coats. Because it was cheaper to buy coats from clothing manufacturers, the drug firm closed down its tailoring division. Similarly, comparison of transfer prices with prices on outside markets led a manufacturer of turbines to hire outside carpenters rather than use its own workers to lay a floor, and led a candy maker to expand its chocolate powder capacity beyond the needs of its other divisions. This is not to say that rational choices about the allocation of the firm's resources cannot be made without transfer prices. But they do sometimes make the alternatives clear.

However, while explicit prices at every stage of production can provide information that is valuable in evaluating performance and making rational decisions, the transactions cost of this type of coordinating mechanism may be very high. Negotiating transfer prices in itself uses up resources (especially workers' time) and, if transfer prices are not equal to marginal costs, then decisions based on them will not be optimal. Furthermore, transfer prices may not reflect all of the costs and benefits to both buyer and seller: just as a merger of two firms may internalize an externality, the divisionalization of an enterprise may create externalities that are not efficiently handled by a price mechanism. Chapter 4 focuses on the efficiency implications of this enterprise structure.

What Is an Enterprise?

The extensive autonomy of the divisions raises a fundamental question: if its subdivisions have so much independence, what then is an enterprise? In the Yugoslav context it cannot be defined in terms of the traditional capitalist firm: we cannot identify a particular group of assets over which ownership is packaged as a coherent unit or a group of activities that is controlled by a single command hierarchy. Coase (1937, p. 322) defined the firm as an 'island of conscious power' that is distinguished by 'the suppression of the price mechanism', and Arrow (1964, p. 403) defined the firm as an organization bounded by a line across which price-mediated transactions take place. Both of these definitions suggest that each division is itself an enterprise. But in Yugoslavia it is usually a collection of divisions that is viewed, by people both inside and outside the group, as an enterprise, a unit that does have some meaning.

In this section I argue that in a number of ways the divisions of a Yugoslav enterprise are not entirely independent of one another. Since there are some ties, since the relationship between two divisions that are in the same firm is different from the relationship between two divisions that are not, the enterprise is a meaningful economic unit. In chapter 4 we shall see that the behavior implied by these intrafirm relationships has important implications for the efficiency of Yugoslav enterprise structure. It is, however, very difficult to find an operational definition of the enterprise, and I am forced to say that an enterprise is any group of divisions that call themselves an enterprise or behave as though they are one. In most cases that behavior consists of some form of collusion, most often market sharing and joint decision-making.[7]

A group of divisions join together for some mutual benefit. They may see some advantage in joint production, marketing or purchasing, or in sharing bookkeeping, computer or personnel services, etc. Often there is a strong desire for stability and a fear of market fluctuations that lead them to try to establish stable supply channels and stable output demand and to dampen price fluctuations. They will enter into relationships with other divisions in the same enterprise and continue to honor and renew these agreements even when external prices are somewhat more attractive. This is not simply a matter of long-term contracts: any two divisions can make a long-term contract and that by itself does not mean that they become an enterprise. Indeed, legally the contracts between divisions within a firm are *not* long-term; usually transfer prices, if not other terms of the agreement, are negotiated annually. Rather, what binds the subunits of an enterprise together is a feeling that 'we're all one family' (a phrase I often heard in Yugoslav firms).

To some extent this results from social and political pressures that encourage 'solidarity' among the divisions of an enterprise. Thus, while each division in principle has the right to buy and sell outside, there is often sufficient local Party and social pressure to deal with a sister division that it will do so as long as the gap between transfer price and external price does not exceed some threshold. Similarly, while each has the right to choose its own outputs, there may be an understanding that specialization will lead to market sharing. Such understanding is often tacit but may be quite explicit, as in a case where a division withdrew from Energoinvest, claiming another division had violated a rule by building facilities to produce an identical product (*Nova Makedonija*, 3 February, 1977, p. 2). Another bond is the fact that, despite the ostensible legal autonomy of the divisions in an enterprise, they often choose to establish mutual liability for debts. Also contributing to the sense of enterprise solidarity is a system of income sharing that is sometimes used to tie intermediate prices to the price of some final product, although such systems are not limited to the subunits of a single enterprise.

In some cases there is an explicit transfer of resources: one division will invest directly in another for purposes of modernization or expansion. Whether the intention is to correct serious production inefficiencies or merely to allow the borrower to take advantage of a profitable opportunity, this raises the thorniest issue of current Yugoslav economic policy, an issue about which both written laws and oral explanations from Yugoslav economists are highly ambiguous. The basic question is whether, and to what extent, a division that supplies capital has a right to share the profits of the division that borrows. The general rule seems to be that the money supplied is treated as a loan that is to be repaid with a rate of interest that is agreed upon in advance. However, the law, as well as the popular press, emphasizes the importance of the principles of 'pooling resources' and 'sharing risks'. Indeed, the law specifies that the investor shall be compensated 'in proportion to the income realized' by the project (LAL, article 84). This seems to mean that the harder the borrowers work, and hence the more successful they are, the greater will be the income of other workers (the investors) who are not actually working in that division. Many observers would call this exploitation. Horvat (1976, p. 170), for example, argues that 'if a person or a group of persons are earning non-labor income, they are exploiting others'.

There are two ways in which this situation can be reconciled with the fundamental socialist principle that prohibits one worker from appropriating the results of the work of another. First, the Yugoslavs consistently refer to the funds supplied as the 'past labor' of the investor. Thus, by contributing funds that they earned with their own labor, the investors have legitimately earned a right to share in whatever profits come from the joint project. Second, the law specifies that profit sharing based on contributed capital may not continue on a permanent basis. A repayment schedule must be set out in advance and once the initial investment is repaid (with interest) the investor's right to a profit share expires (LAL, articles 83–6). While the wording of the law is ambiguous, it seems that this could not mean that the right to a profit share expires as soon as the cumulative sum of profits received equals the initial investment (plus interest). If it did, the investor would in fact be receiving a fixed return, and the profitability of the project would determine only the rapidity with which the funds are repaid. Instead, the law is being interpreted to mean that until the loan is repaid the investor is contributing resources to the project and hence has a right to a share of profits *in addition to* the eventual return of his invested funds with interest. The details of several examples of such arrangements are examined in chapter 6.

While interdivisional lending is not a new concept, the recent increases in divisional autonomy and the virtual elimination of any enterprise funds or central authority to transfer funds between divisions have very much increased the importance of this aspect of enterprise structure. One might argue that on theoretical grounds profit sharing is better (less capitalistic) than the debtor–creditor relationship implied by a fixed return; or one might argue the opposite. But in either case the increased mobility of capital that results from the additional incentive to lend seems certain to improve the overall efficiency of resource allocation. Indeed, capital immobility has long been a problem in theoretical studies of self-managed economic systems (see, for example, Vanek, 1970, especially part IV). Chapter 5 examines the theory of investment decisions in divisionalized firms, but at this point a more empirical perspective is appropriate.

It should be made clear that interdivisional loans with variable returns is not the only way in which divisions can share risks. As mentioned above, in some enterprises transfer prices are stated not as a fixed number of dinars per unit, but as a percentage of the selling price of the final product. Thus all of the divisions have an interest in the price, as well as in the quantity, of the final good sold.

In practice, the real incentive to invest in another division is almost always the increased availability of some input (usually at a lower price) or increased demand for some output. This is true even when the investor and borrower are in different enterprises. For example, a shoe manufacturer in Zagreb contributed to the costs of expansion of a slaughterhouse that was not part of its enterprise. Its reason for making the investment was to expand the domestic supply of leather, and the agreement provided for no explicit profit sharing. Similarly, three separate chemical enterprises in Serbia jointly financed construction of a lead and zinc mine that will supply them with needed inputs, and a new factory for manufacturing cathode ray tubes was financed by Elektronska Industrija, ISKRA, RIZ and other makers of television sets. In this and a few other cases the financing crosses republican boundaries. For example, Sava, a Slovenian firm, and Energoinvest, in Bosnia and Hercegovina, jointly financed a synthetic rubber factory.

Investment projects undertaken jointly by several divisions can be conceptually quite complex. Figure 1.1 depicts a situation that required the advice of several economists experienced in advising firms on how to structure themselves so as to meet the requirements of the new Law on Associated Labor. Two Belgrade enterprises jointly founded a new division that was to be a constituent part of one of the founders. Enterprise M is a manufacturing firm, and Enterprise C is a commercial firm engaged largely in importing and exporting. The new

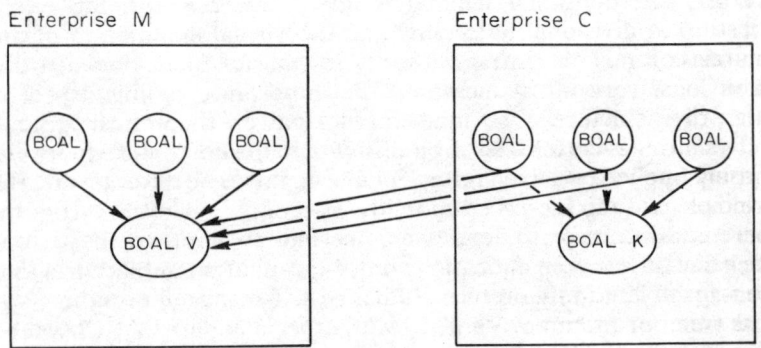

Arrows indicate capital flow

Figure 1.1

division, indicated by V on the diagram, will manufacture a plastic part. Enterprise M (or, more precisely, its three pre-existing constituent divisions) provided 40 per cent of the capital for the new division and Enterprise C (that is, its divisions) provided the other 60 per cent. The total capital contributed was $12 million. Also founded was a new division within Enterprise C. This new division (labeled K) will import various inputs to be sold to division V and will handle sales of the new plastic part. Resources necessary for founding division K were minimal (some office space, a few typewriters and about twenty employees) and were provided entirely by the pre-existing divisions of Enterprise C.

What is interesting about this type of situation is that, once founded, the new divisions are legally autonomous. They must repay the loans that provided their initial capital according to whatever terms were set, but once they begin operation their capital is technically their own. Legally, there is nothing to prevent a newly founded division, like any other division, from withdrawing from the enterprise, i.e. taking its recently supplied capital and running away. (Of course, it cannot avoid repaying the loans.) Indeed, it is this very fact that prevents the founder(s) from imposing exploitative transfer prices. The establishment of a new division is likely to take place only if it promises to be advantageous to all parties concerned.

Perhaps the most important bond tying together the divisions in an enterprise is the enterprise plan. Annually, representatives of every division jointly work out detailed plans (now called self-management agreements) for the coming year. (There are also supposed to be five-year plans.) Agreements are made specifying exactly which goods and services each division is to produce; delivery dates and quantities are set; and transfer prices are settled. Once approved by all the constituent divisions, the enterprise plan becomes a set of legally binding contracts. A division's right to withdraw from the enterprise or to buy or sell outside is conditional on its fulfilling its obligations to the other divisions as specified in the enterprise plan.

The increasing emphasis on economic planning, which was evident throughout Yugoslav society in the 1970s, appears to conflict with the principle of autonomy for the divisions. Yet the Yugoslavs deny that there is any conflict: as long as there is no central office (either inside the enterprise or outside) with authority to impose production decisions, each division is merely making its own decisions in consultation with other economic units. It is in this respect like French indicative planning. (But within Yugoslav enterprises plans are more precise and the parties to the agreement actually sign a contract.) An underlying principle is that the sharing of information is in itself highly desirable because it will enable a market mechanism to work more smoothly.

16 Self-Management and Efficiency: Large Corporations in Yugoslavia

One way of viewing planning in the Yugoslav system is as a set of forward markets (Schrenk et al., 1979, p. 78). Buyers and sellers negotiate quantities and prices in advance so that future relative scarcities become known. Meade (1970, p. 3) argues that 'forward markets and indicative planning are in fact information systems which reduce uncertainty by passing to producers the knowledge which consumers have about future demand conditions and passing to consumers the knowledge which producers have about future supply conditions.' He shows (1970, pp. 23–8) that a complete set of forward markets (including conditional contracts) or elaborate indicative planning (including separate contingency plans) can result in Pareto optimality with all conditional future spot markets in equilibrium at forecasted prices. The major problem in Yugoslavia, of course, is that, in the absence of a complete set of contingency markets, adjustments will have to be made by way of spot markets when the environment determines important exogenous factors that were uncertain at the time the forward contracts were concluded. The efficiency of overall resource allocation in such a situation will depend on the divisions' technological ability to adjust production plans and on their legal flexibility to renegotiate contracts.

This joint planning by a number of divisions is viewed by many Yugoslavs as the key distinguishing characteristic of the enterprise. But it is in fact not an operational distinction because there is also inter-enterprise planning. All of the enterprises in an industry (as well as their suppliers and customers) are expected to formulate self-management agreements concerning future production plans so as to avoid bottlenecks or the idle capacity that can result from overinvestment. Thus, while some plans are more specific than others, we cannot define the enterprise in terms of which divisions make joint plans.

It seems that we cannot in the abstract identify the enterprise. Some groups of divisions are more closely tied together than others in terms of decision-making, sharing facilities and services, income distribution, joint investment and the degree of detail of their planning. Even more important, we can observe that divisions that are in the same enterprise display certain behavior toward one another. In addition to market sharing, they often show a greater concern for each other's financial condition. A division is less likely to take some action (say, cancelling an order, demanding a better price or dropping an item from its product line) if it will harm a sister division rather than a separate firm. On the basis of such structural and behavioral criteria, some groups can rightly be called enterprises; but only someone familiar with a particular working relationship can say whether that particular group of divisions should be considered an enterprise, that is, a meaningful economic unit. If two 'enterprises' began to engage in reasonably tight coordination of facilities, investment, planning and income sharing, then I would say the entire group of divisions becomes an enterprise. For example, Industrija Nafta (INA), Yugoslavia's largest corporation, consists of seventy-eight divisions grouped into fourteen 'enterprises'. I would argue that the ties among its constituent parts are sufficiently strong that INA should be viewed as a single enterprise, a large and complex one with considerable divisional autonomy, but an enterprise nonetheless. Indeed, on the Yugoslav equivalent of the *Fortune* '500' list,[8] it is treated so (although it is mentioned that some of its parts would themselves qualify for position on the list).

It is worth noting that while the word 'enterprise' (*preduzeće*) is no longer officially used in Yugoslavia, the terms 'work organization' and 'organization of associated labor' (OAL), which refer to a group of divisions that have joined together, are often translated as 'enterprise' and informally Yugoslavs often refer to an OAL as an enterprise. There is a third term, 'complex organization of associated labor' (COAL), which consists of two or more OALs that have joined together (Connor and Vukmir, 1976). The question is, which term should be translated as 'enterprise'? In many cases this is merely a semantic question, but in some situations it causes serious problems for empirical research. If we are interested in studying the functioning of the market mechanism in Yugoslavia, we may want to examine, for instance, concentration ratios or the extent of vertical integration. Such concepts are meaningless without some notion of what an enterprise is and how many of them there are. One must decide how to interpret official statistics on the 'number of organizations' in the industrial sector. As explained in chapter 2 (note 3), the Statistical Institute has not been consistent in its methodology. In the middle years of the 1970s it sometimes counted individual divisions (BOALs) and sometimes the larger groupings (OALs or COALs) of which they are a part. It now counts divisions. This would be appropriate if divisions were always entirely independent entities, but we know that they are often members of enterprises in which they not only share resources but also engage in market sharing, price fixing and other forms of collusion. Of course, divisions can share costs without being part of the same enterprise (after all, totally separate firms essentially share the costs of producing electricity when they buy from the same power company), just as they can collude without being part of the same firm. Conversely, divisions that *are* part of the same enterprise can compete (as do several Zagreb breweries that continue to compete after having merged). But both cost sharing and reduced competition are more likely when divisions combine to form a single enterprise.

Before concluding this chapter, I should point out that the practice of creating autonomous subunits within large enterprises is not new, nor did it originate with the Yugoslavs, although they have carried it further than any other country. In the United States, divisionalization into relatively autonomous units was first implemented in large enterprises by DuPont and General Motors (GM) in the 1920s. In 1927 Donaldson Brown at GM ordered that 'whether the products of a division went to other General Motors divisions or outside, they were sold at the going market price'. Further, he encouraged some outside purchases of goods made within the firm 'so as to perfect the competitive situation' (Chandler, 1962, p. 144). Standard Oil of New Jersey and Sears and Roebuck also divisionalized early, but most large American firms did not follow along until somewhat later. During the period 1949–69 the divisionalized structure became the dominant organizational form in large American firms and in 1981 the principle was reaffirmed at its source: GM chairman Roger Smith increased the authority of division heads to make decisions and said he wanted Chevrolet, Buick, Pontiac, Oldsmobile and Cadillac to 'compete as fiercely with one another as with Ford Motor Company or Chrysler Corporation' (*Wall Street Journal*, 21 May, 1981, pp. 29 and 41). Recently, the concept of divisionalization has been adopted by large Western European firms and can even be seen in changes taking place in the socialist countries of Eastern Europe and the Soviet Union (see chapter 7). Oliver Williamson claims (1970, p. 175) that development of the multidivisional corporation, along with certain internal control apparatus, may be 'American capitalism's most important single innovation of the 20th century'.

While the structure of Yugoslav enterprises is in many ways similar to divisionalized American firms, there is no reason to suppose that they were created for the same reasons. On the contrary, according to Williamson American firms adopted the divisionalized structure because growth was causing a loss of control on the part of the central management. The restructuring was seen as a way of reducing two types of control loss: (1) faulty or incomplete flow of information up the hierarchy and of commands down the hierarchy, and (2) deliberate pursuit of subunit goals (e.g. expansion, autarky or even a leisurely pace of work) that do not always coincide with the goals of the overall enterprise. Thus, divisionalization was introduced to *improve* the center's control over large and often diversified firms. The innovators sought to free top executives from day-to-day operating decisions so that they could devote more attention to such long-run matters as the allocation of existing resources and the acquisition of additional resources (Williamson, 1970, pp. 113–17).

By contrast, it can hardly be said that changes in the structure of Yugoslav enterprises were intended to improve central control.

Milenkovitch (1977, pp. 56, 57 and 59) tells us that the purpose of decentralization was 'to reduce the importance of the managerial and financial elite . . .' and to 'weaken the central administration of the enterprises' so as to achieve the 'worker participation' and 'direct control' necessary for genuine self-management. The underlying belief is that meaningful worker participation is possible only if small work units (the subunits of the enterprise) have considerable autonomy.

While the decentralization of Yugoslav enterprises did relieve top executives of the need to make day-to-day operating decisions, at the same time it deprived them of the authority to make the long-run strategic decisions that their western counterparts concentrate on. Indeed, numerous Yugoslav jokes are based on the assertion that central management has nothing whatsoever to do. However, such jokes are misleading. In fact, Yugoslav as well as western top executives do evaluate current activities and plan new ones. They do make decisions regarding the allocation of existing resources and the acquisition of additional resources. The difference is that, since they lack the authority to impose their decisions, they must convince the representatives of the various subunits to accept them. The Yugoslav executive must be more of a political animal than his American counterpart and his success depends very much on his ability to persuade.

Summary

Many businessmen and some economists fear that Yugoslav enterprises are being shattered into uncoordinated fragments. Other observers claim that divisional autonomy is mere show and that central managers retain real control. While one must be careful not to exaggerate, the fact is that the divisions do have very substantial autonomy in deciding what to produce, where to obtain inputs and where to sell outputs. The Yugoslav economic philosophy of self-management by small work units is being implemented to a very considerable extent.

An autonomous division is created whenever the performance of a group of workers can meaningfully be measured in terms of value. Divisions deal with other divisions, both within and between enterprises, by buying and selling goods and services at prices negotiated between them. A division always has the right to deal with divisions outside its own firm, and may even withdraw from the firm. The incomes of workers depend primarily on the performance of their own division, although there are other influences as well. Within an enterprise, wage differentials do not exactly measure divisional performance, but workers in divisions that are performing well earn more than those in divisions that are doing poorly.

An important aspect of the relationship among the divisions within an enterprise is the prices at which they trade. These transfer prices do affect production decisions, as well as the distribution of income within the firm. Furthermore, in most cases they approximate external market prices, although sometimes they are adjusted to favor a weak division, repay a loan or reflect changes in the price of a final product. In a number of specific instances there is evidence that the use of transfer prices has led to a rational reallocation of a firm's resources. However, there are some situations in which transfer prices do not reflect true marginal cost and hence may lead to inefficient firm behavior. Further, the time and effort necessary to negotiate transfer prices may make this mechanism costly to use. Chapter 4 takes up the question of the efficiency of this enterprise structure.

The fact that the divisions of an enterprise are legally independent does not necessarily mean that their activities are uncoordinated. There is an elaborate system of annual planning in which the separate divisions enter into agreements about future activities. The Yugoslavs prefer to call this polycentric planning; but since decisions are made by a large number of independent actors, rather than by some central authority with effective controls, it is essentially a market mechanism, wherein contracts provide the necessary coordination of independent activities.

There are also a number of other factors that tie together the divisions of an enterprise. One important consideration is the sense of solidarity, of being part of one family, that often leads a division to buy from or sell to another division in the same enterprise even when an outside price is more favorable. Or transfer prices may be adjusted so that the income of each division varies with the price of a final product. Often funds are invested by one division in another under an agreement that requires that one supply the other, at least until the investment costs are repaid. Perhaps most important is the fact that in Yugoslavia the market mechanism operating inside the enterprise is somewhat different from that operating between enterprises: a sense of internal solidarity facilitates joint decision-making and collusion among divisions within a firm, thus making market sharing and price fixing more likely. This reduces the likelihood of wasteful duplication of capacity, but also threatens the effectiveness of competition.

In the next chapter I examine the size of enterprises and their divisions.

Notes

1 See, for example, Hirshleifer (1956, 1957), Dean (1955), Baumol and Fabian (1964), Heflebower (1960), Dearden (1962) and Cook (1955). David Granick has done work on international comparisons of the use of transfer prices; see, for example, Granick (1975b).
2 For detailed discussion of some of the early legal developments see Sacks (1973), especially pp. 10–14 and 62–4.
3 While in principle the enterprise is formed by the voluntary joining together of its constituent parts, in practice the immediate task created by the new Constitution (1974) and the Law on Associated Labor (1976) was to redefine the subunits of existing enterprises so as to meet the specific requirements of the new law. In many cases this meant increasing the number of subunits.
4 Details of two of these examples appeared in newspapers: *Borba*, 7 January, 1977, p. 6, and 5 April, 1977, p. 2, and *Nova Makedonija*, 3 February, 1977, p. 2. I learned about the RIZ case in a personal interview at RIZ.
5 Constitution (1974), article 36 and repeated verbatim in Basic Law on Associated Labor, article 14. See also articles 410 and 411 of that Law.
6 This view of the determination and importance of transfer prices, as well as my view of the degree of independence of divisions, is different from that of David Granick (1975a). This difference is probably due to the fact that his work is based on interviews conducted in 1970 and 1971, before adoption of major laws that emphasize subunit autonomy. For a third view see Schrenk *et al.* (1979).
7 While this book was in press I came across the following statement by a respected authority on the theory of the firm: 'I shall then argue that we do not exactly know what the firm is . . . The word "firm" is simply a shorthand description of a way to organize activities under contractual arrangements that differ from those of ordinary product markets.' (Cheung, 1983, p. 3) He is, of course, referring to conventional capitalist firms.
8 *Ekonomska Politika*'s list of the 130 largest industrial enterprises.

2 Giant Corporations in Yugoslavia

> Forces inherent in labor-management are infinitely less likely to lead to inordinate concentrations of industrial power ... [and a] labor-managed industrial conglomerate is as likely an occurrence as the apocalyptic beast with seven heads and ten horns.
> (Vanek, 1970, pp. 287–8)

The above quotation is the most dramatic of several statements that Vanek makes in asserting that there 'is a far lesser danger of gigantism – and a corresponding far greater likelihood of competitive conditions – in labor-managed market structures than in just about any other economic regime' (Vanek, 1970, p. 119). The purpose of this chapter is to examine empirical evidence from the Yugoslav economy to determine whether very large corporations have in fact evolved in this labor-managed system.

The chapter begins with a discussion of the importance of enterprise size for the functioning of the Yugoslav economy. There follows a brief review of Vanek's theoretical basis for his assertion that 'the equilibrium size of a labor-managed firm is considerably smaller than that of a capitalist firm' (Vanek, 1970, p. 105). The bulk of the chapter consists of presentation and discussion of the empirical evidence. The evidence falls into two categories, that which deals with whole enterprises and that which deals with divisions.

The Significance of Large Firms

Before turning to the theoretical and empirical discussion of the size of Yugoslav firms, it is worth considering some of the reasons for believing that firm size is important to the operation of the Yugoslav economy. That importance depends in part on the fact that the Yugoslav economy is essentially a market system, although some observers would argue that it is not. During the latter part of the 1960s and the early 1970s the Yugoslavs became disenchanted with the market mechanism and began to mistrust it. Many thought it led to instability, inequality and inefficient use of resources. The idea of planning became popular, but few Yugoslavs wanted to return to the central planning system of the immediate post-war period. Instead of totally abandoning the market mechanism, Yugoslavia has tried to synthesize a unique system that includes both the market and decentralized planning. The fundamental characteristic of the resulting system is numerous independent decision-makers exchanging goods and services for money, that is, market transactions. It is true that self-management agreements sometimes tie buyers and sellers for a number of years and may set specific criteria for determining prices. Often the relationship between buyer and seller is complicated by prices that vary according to specified circumstances, by investment relationships, and by various sorts of risk sharing. Often the federal and republic governments set prices. Certainly, this is not a pure market economy. But if it were not *primarily* a market system then the market would have to be, to a substantial extent, *replaced* by planning, and it is difficult to argue that there is much *effective* planning in Yugoslavia beyond some thinking ahead by independent actors. In any market system the participants plan their own future actions and negotiate contracts in advance for some period of time. General Motors does not decide every morning which cars to produce today and from whom to buy headlights for that day's production. Planning means taking some action to affect the outcome of events. In Yugoslavia there is no *effective, comprehensive* mechanism for influencing the allocation of resources. Whatever planning there is is done within the context of a market by the participants in that market.

Milenkovitch (1977, p. 58) describes the planning mechanism as 'agonizingly vague', and Schrenck, who seems to think the planning process is meaningful, admits (Schrenck *et al.*, 1979, p. 76) that 'no common and rigorous methodology of self-management planning has emerged'. He describes a system of 'planning' that takes place everywhere simultaneously and continuously and that involves no hierarchy; plans are revised whenever necessary and are accepted only when all parties agree. This may be called planning and may involve participants going through certain motions, but it is essentially a market system with contracts. Of course, the openness that comes from widespread discussions may indeed facilitiate the harmonization of different activities, but that is no different from saying that information improves the working of a market.

The important point is that much of what we know about the workings of a market is relevant to a study of the Yugoslav economy. In particular, it is true, although perhaps not obvious, that concern with the influence of large corporations on the effectiveness of competition is no less relevant in this socialist country than it is in a capitalist framework. Regardless of who owns the banks and the means of production and regardless of how profits are distributed, if an economy relies on market forces to ensure technical and allocative efficiency, then effective competition is necessary for proper functioning of the system. Whether the socialist firm maximizes total profit, profit per worker or some Galbraithian maximand like size or stability, if the system is designed to rely on the discipline of competition it will work less well in the presence of large firms if they are free of that discipline. Similarly, regardless of their own optimization rules, if socialist firms learn that relatively large size confers advantages in the competitive process, then they, as well as capitalist firms, may expand beyond the size necessary to exhaust physical economies of scale in production.

While the vigor of competition is not necessarily proportional to the number of competitors, effective operation of any market system does require at least a few firms, and for a given size market the presence of larger firms means there is room for fewer others. This is particularly important in a country where the total size of markets is small. To some extent it is possible to rely on foreign firms to provide the necessary competitive pressure. Indeed, since 1965 official Yugoslav policy has been to reduce tariffs and encourage international trade, in part for this very reason. However, balance of payments problems and pressure from special interest groups have hindered the implementation of this policy and in many industries effective competition requires that there be a number of domestic firms.

In addition to the obvious effect on the number of competitors, there are other considerations. Hart and Prais (1956), for example, discuss the influence of relatively large firms on the effectiveness of competition, emphasizing certain advantages they have over their smaller competitors, such as easier access to capital and lower per unit costs of advertising and distribution, as well as economies of scale in direct production costs. These advantages reduce the pressures that, in the microeconomic theory of the market system, drive average cost down toward its minimum and price down toward average cost. As relative size differences decrease, however, these advantages tend to disappear. Hence, effective competition (that is, competition that does in fact reduce the gap between price and average cost) is more likely among firms of approximately equal size. The essence of this argument is that the market mechanism works best when every firm perceives a threat that other firms will lure away customers by selling at a lower price, and that this threat is less credible to firms with cost advantages due to size. There are, of course, many other influences on price–cost margins.

The significance of large firm size for effective competition is clearest in cases where firms are large relative to other firms in a particular market – that is, where their size gives them a large share of a well-defined market. However, size relative to *all* other firms (not just those in the same industry) also has significance for the effectiveness of competition. The two most important ways in which large absolute size interferes with competitiveness involve access to capital and what is called *reciprocity*. In an ideally functioning market system, a firm's ability to attract capital suppliers and customers depends entirely upon the price and quality of the product or service it sells. However, banks often are more willing to lend, or to lend at a lower interest rate, to a large conglomerate simply because it is large (perhaps because banks believe that the risk is lower when the borrower is large or diversified). This puts smaller firms or potential entrants at a disadvantage. Reciprocity refers to a situation where a division of a large conglomerate acquires customers, not because of the prices or quality of its products, but because other divisions (or customers or suppliers of other divisions) have been pressured to buy from it. For example, the US Department of Justice accused Ling-Temco-Vought of pressuring General Motors to buy steel from an LTV-owned steel producer under threat that an LTV-owned car rental agency would buy its cars from Ford or Chrysler.

In a broader sense, large size (which may or may not entail a large share of individual markets) can be said to be important per se, because every firm is a potential entrant to other markets and every product competes for the consumer's money (see Triffin, 1940, pp. 88–9). Hart and Prais (1956, p. 152) claim that if 'large firms today control a greater part of the resources of the economy in relation to the remaining firms than they used to ... there is a *prima facie* case for saying that opportunities for monopolistic practices are increasing in individual industries'.

Furthermore, when economic systems are compared, certain advantages of a competitive market system over command and traditional economies are often discussed. Among them is the fact that society's output mix is more the result of impersonal forces of supply and demand, reflecting a large number of individual consumption and production decisions, than of the decisions of some relatively small group of people. This characteristic is often considered desirable in itself on political grounds (that is, as a limitation on the concentration of power), as well as for its contribution to the efficiency of resource allocation. But as firms grow they draw into themselves transactions that would otherwise be handled in a marketplace by negotiation between separate decision-makers. The possibility that such growth may lead to an increasing concentration of power in a capitalist system has been a matter of concern for many years (Berle and Means, 1932). More recently, White (1981a, p. 224) has referred to aggregate concentration as a measure 'which would allow us to make inferences about the concentration of political and social power'. (See also Feinberg, 1981, and White, 1981b.) But the problem is not unique to capitalism. One of the advantages claimed for market socialism, over the alternative of centralized (or Soviet-type) socialism, is its broad dispersion of decision-making power. Thus the growth of giant corporations may violate a fundamental principle of decentralized socialism.

One might argue that under the Yugoslav form of socialism the principle of worker self-management so broadens the decision-making process within the firm that the number or relative size of firms is unimportant: each worker has a proportionate voice in the decision-making of his firm. However, two problems remain. First, the decisions of some workers will have a relatively greater impact on the economy than the decisions of others if sales per worker or assets per worker are greater in large firms than in small firms. Second, while something like a market mechanism is used to govern transactions among the divisions of a single firm, with respect to other firms workers act in their collective interest – that is, they collude. The economy's output mix, then, results from the production decisions of workers acting in collusive groups, rather than independently.

Theory of Firm Size

Before examining the empirical evidence, we might ask what firm size we would expect to find in Yugoslavia. Vanek's theoretical analysis is built on the now well-known principle that a labor-managed firm will hire workers up to the point where the marginal revenue product of labor falls just enough to equal the average income per worker.[1] At lower levels of labor input, an additional worker would add more to enterprise income than he takes as his share of the total; thus, adding a worker would raise the income of the other workers. Conversely, at higher levels of labor input, reducing the labor force by one worker would reduce total revenue by less than the income share that would have gone to that worker; thus, reducing the labor force would raise the average income of the remaining workers. An important characteristic of this optimum level of labor input is that it corresponds to the bottom of the short-run average cost curve, or what Vanek calls the point of maximum physical efficiency, because it maximizes output per worker for the given fixed amount of capital.

By contrast, a capitalist 'twin' with the same amount of capital might choose to hire more workers and produce more output. It will continue to hire until the marginal revenue product of labor falls to the price of labor, which, if there is excess profit being made, is lower than the income share of a worker in the labor-managed firm. That is, a declining marginal revenue product curve will intersect the price of labor curve to the right (that is, at a higher level of labor input and hence of output) of its intersection with the curve that represents total income of a worker who gets profit share as well as wage. That it has gone beyond the bottom of its average cost curve does not matter to the capitalist firm, which is interested in maximizing not average or marginal profit but total profit.

Vanek expands this analysis of input and output decisions to the case where the amount of capital as well as labor is variable. The concept of maximum physical efficiency then corresponds to a locus of capital–labor combinations, corresponding to the bottom points of different long-run average cost curves, representing various factor price combinations. This locus can be projected as a contour on the production function surface, where it marks the separation between the region of increasing returns and the region of decreasing returns. Just as in the case where the quantity of capital is assumed fixed, the labor-managed firm, being interested in maximizing the value of output *per worker*, will not expand beyond the locus of maximum physical efficiency. In fact, if it has some monopoly power it will stop expanding before reaching that locus, that is, within the range of increasing returns. The capitalist firm, however, being interested in *total* profit, may choose to produce at an output level beyond that locus; that is, it may go beyond the minimum point on its average cost curve. Indeed, it will operate at the bottom of its average cost curve only under perfect competition. If the price of the product and the capitalist's cost of labor are such as to allow the capitalist firm to earn excess profit, then it will choose a higher output level than the labor-managed 'twin'. Vanek's conclusion is that 'the impetus to grow indefinitely, and thus to control a sizeable portion of the market, in the labor-managed firm can be expected to be considerably less than in the case of its capitalist equivalent' (Vanek, 1970, p. 34). This view that, except for perfect competition, self-managed firms will use less labor and produce less output than similar capitalist firms is widely accepted in the theoretical literature. See, for example, Meade (1972, 1974), Atkinson (1973) and Milenkovitch (1983). Steinherr (1975, p. 104), too, concludes that in many cases 'market structures will be more competitive in a labor-managed economy'.

Some Empirical Evidence

Data on Yugoslavia's large firms are published annually by *Ekonomska Politika*, a weekly news magazine. This equivalent of the

Table 2.1

(a) Number of industrial firms with more than x workers

	1969	1970	1971	1972	1973	1974	1975	1976	1977	1978	1979	1980	1981
$x = 10{,}000$	12	20	23	25	27	30	37	43	50	50	48	54	57
$x = 20{,}000$	1	2	6	8	8	10	11	12	13	16	15	15	17
$x = 30{,}000$	0	0	1	1	1	3	3	5	5	5	5	5	8

(b) Number of trade sector firms with more than x workers

	1969	1970	1971	1972	1973	1974	1975	1976	1977	1978	1979	1980	1981
$x = 5{,}000$	0	3	4	5	5	6	10	12	11	15	15	16	15
$x = 10{,}000$	0	0	1	1	1	3	3	2	3	3	5	6	8

Source: Calculated from data taken from *Ekonomska Politika*, various issues.

Table 2.2

(a) *Industrial workers employed in firms with more than x workers*

		1969	1970	1971	1972	1973	1974	1975	1976	1977	1978	1979	1980	1981
$x = 10{,}000$	No.	171	308	379	436	481	551	680	790	926	940	931	1032	1137
	%	8	15	17	19	20	22	27	31	33	32	31	33	35
$x = 20{,}000$	No.	22	46	142	194	217	273	319	358	416	470	477	491	568
	%	1	2	6	8	9	11	13	14	15	16	16	16	18
$x = 30{,}000$	No.	0	0	33	34	48	113	118	188	216	211	226	233	345
	%	0	0	1	1	2	5	5	7	8	7	7	7	11

No. = number of workers (in thousands).
% = number of workers as percentage of total industrial labor force.

(b) *Trade sector workers employed in firms with more than x workers*

		1969	1970	1971	1972	1973	1974	1975	1976	1977	1978	1979	1980	1981
$x = 5{,}000$	No.	0	25	33	42	39	59	85	97	102	148	156	174	173
	%	0	6	7	9	8	11	14	15	15	21	21	22	22
$x = 10{,}000$	No.	0	0	16	18	15	40	41	27	43	56	81	97	120
	%	0	0	3	4	3	7	7	4	6	8	11	12	15

No. = number of workers (in thousands).
% = number of workers as percentage of total trade sector labor force.

Source: Calculated from data taken from *Ekonomska Politika*, various issues.

Fortune '500' list includes sales, assets and number of employees for the 100–200 largest enterprises in the country. The number of firms covered has increased over the years since the list was first published for 1968.[2] The analysis and conclusions that follow are based on the lists for 1969–81, and focus primarily on the 100 largest industrial firms and the 50 largest trade enterprises.

The size of Yugoslavia's large enterprises is evident in Tables 2.1 and 2.2, which I have calculated using the *Ekonomska Politika* lists. From Table 2.1(a) one can see that in 1981 there were fifty-seven industrial firms that employed more than 10,000 workers each. Seventeen of these firms employed over 20,000 workers, and eight had over 30,000 workers. In the trade sector (Table 2.1(b)) that year there were fifteen firms with over 5,000 employees, of which eight firms had over 10,000 workers. Looking across the rows, one can see that in nearly every year the number of firms above each size threshold increases, indicating a steady growth in the size of Yugoslavia's largest firms.

Table 2.2 shows the importance of these large firms relative to the rest of the economy. For example, in 1981 industrial firms with over 10,000 workers employed a total of 1,137,000 workers or 35 per cent of the total industrial labor force. Exactly half of those workers (568,000 or 18 per cent of the industrial labor force) worked in firms with over 20,000 employees. Eleven per cent of the industrial labor force (345,000 workers) worked in firms with over 30,000 workers. In the trade sector in 1981, 22 per cent and 15 per cent of that sector's labor force worked in firms with over 5,000 workers and 10,000 workers, respectively.

Over the period 1969–81 the percentage of the industrial labor force working in firms with over 10,000 employees more than quadrupled (from 8 per cent to 35 per cent), while the percentage in firms with over 20,000 workers increased from 1 per cent to 18 per cent. Similar steady increases are evident in Table 2.2(b) for the trade sector.

A similar picture emerges if one looks at the *Ekonomska Politika* data in a different way. Figure 2.1(a) shows the share of total industrial sector economic activity accounted for by the largest fifty firms (ranked by sales). Two important characteristics are noticeable immediately: these 50 firms account for a substantial share of the industrial sector, and their share of economic activity has been rising steadily over the period 1969–81. In 1969 the fifty largest industrial firms accounted for 16 per cent of the sector's workers, 25 per cent of its assets, and 26 per cent of total industrial sales. By 1981 these figures had risen to 31 per cent, 49 per cent, and 53 per cent, respectively. Figure 2.1(b) shows the same variables for the entire list of 130 large industrial firms, but covers only 1972–81, because the list was shorter in the early years. By

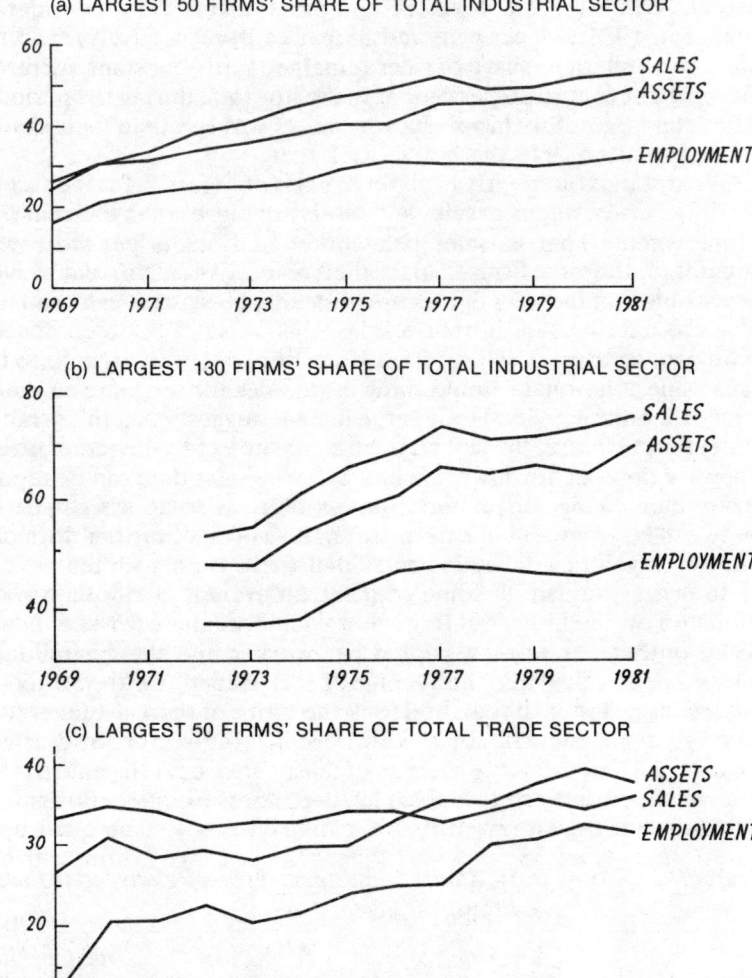

Figure 2.1

1981 the 130 largest firms accounted for 49 per cent of industrial workers, 70 per cent of all industrial assets, and 75 per cent of sector sales.

Figure 2.1(c) shows the largest fifty firms' share of sales, assets and employment in the trade sector. In this case the increases over the period are not as steady as those that are evident in the industrial sector. While the employment and asset shares were considerably higher in 1981 (31 per cent and 38 per cent, respectively) than they were in 1969, their share of sales remained fairly constant, increasing from 34 per cent to 36 per cent of the sector total during the period. In 1969 the largest fifty firms' share of assets was less than their share of sales, but after 1976 the latter was larger.

What stands out clearly in all three parts of Figure 2.1 is the fact that the large firms' shares of sales and assets are bigger than their shares of employment. That is, sales per worker and assets per worker are greater for the large firms than for their respective sectors as a whole. It is possible that the sales figures are misleading because the *Ekonomska Politika* data include intrafirm sales, that is, sales between divisions within an enterprise. If large firms were more finely divisionalized than small ones, their data would show more sales for the same amount of real economic activity. However, evidence suggests that this is not the case. Furthermore, the asset data are not subject to the same bias and they are only slightly lower. In any case, the sales data can be used for examining changes over time, unless there is some systematic bias between large and small enterprises in the speed of further divisionalization. Again, evidence indicates that there is no such bias.

In order to quantify some of these differences, I calculated some statistics on the industrial firms. For each firm and each year I calculated output per worker, capital per worker and the capital/output ratio. Then I calculated the average of each statistic for the 50 and 100 largest firms for each year, and took the ratios of these averages to the corresponding statistic for the entire industrial sector for that year. Shown in Table 2.3 is the average of these ratios over the entire period for which the data are available (1970–81 for the largest 100 firms and 1969–81 for the largest 50).

Table 2.3 *Some Basic Statistics on Large Firms Relative to the Entire Industrial Sector,[a] 1969–81*

	Output per worker	Capital per worker	Capital/output ratio
Largest 100 firms	1.73	1.56	.97
Largest 50 firms	1.86	1.63	.95

[a] Each element in the table is equal to

$$\left(\sum_{i=1}^{n} \frac{\text{average statistic for the group of large firms in year } i}{\text{same statistic for the entire industrial sector in year } i} \right) \div n$$

where n is 12 years for the first row of the table and 13 years for the second row. Notice that by calculating a ratio for each year and then averaging, we get pure numbers and hence avoid any need to adjust for price changes.

For example, the table shows that over the period 1970–81 output per worker averaged 73 per cent higher in the 100 largest industrial firms than in the industrial sector as a whole. This is in part explained by the fact that capital per worker was on average 56 per cent higher in these firms. But this is not simply a matter of more capital: their capital/output ratio averaged 97 per cent of the sector-wide capital/output ratio. Apparently, either these firms use capital more effectively or there is some input not being taken into account here. It is also possible that they use technologies that are not practical for smaller firms or that are distributed differently across industries.

The second row of Table 2.3 shows that if one looks at only the largest fifty firms the contrast with the whole industrial sector is even sharper. Output per worker averages 86 per cent greater than the sector-wide figure, and while the capital per worker statistic is even higher than for the 100 largest firms, the capital/output ratio is slightly better: their capital/output ratio is only 95 per cent of the sector-wide figure. That is, the fifty largest firms average 8 per cent more output per worker than in the largest 100 firms (((1.86 − 1.73) / 1.73 = .08) but have only 4 per cent more capital per worker (((1.63 − 1.56) / 1.56 = .04) than in those firms.

We have noted that large firms account for a very substantial share of total economic activity in Yugoslavia. In fact, their share is so substantial (the 130 largest industrial firms accounted for 75 per cent of total industrial sector sales in 1981) that if we are interested in changing relative firm sizes we must examine data on subgroups within the *Ekonomska Politika* list. In Figure 2.2 I have graphed on the same pair of axes the shares of total industrial sector activity for the largest 50, 100 and 130 industrial firms. This enables us to think in terms of three subgroups, one consisting of the fifty largest firms, one consisting of firms 51–100, and one consisting of firms 101–130. The fact that the middle and upper lines on the graphs appear nearly parallel to the lowest line indicates that the second and third subgroups have retained a fairly constant share of total industrial activity while most of the increase noted earlier is attributable to the first subgroup.

Actually, while the distance between the top and middle lines on the graphs (the third subgroup's share) has remained at between 5 and 6 per cent of industrial sales, assets and employment, the distance between the middle and lower lines did increase somewhat during the period. In terms of sales and assets, the share of the second subgroup increased from 10 per cent to 16 per cent and from 10 per cent to 15 per cent, respectively. In terms of employment, the second subgroup's share increased during the 1970–81 period from 8.5 per cent to 12 per cent. These increases are smaller than the first subgroup's increases over the decade: 27 per cent in sales (from 26 per cent to 53 per cent of the sector total), 24 per cent in assets (from 25 per cent to 49 per cent), and 15 per cent in employment (from 16 per cent of the total to 31 per cent). But they are roughly in proportion to the initial relative sizes of the subgroups. Detailed examination of the underlying data shows that the shares of each subgroup relative to the group of giants as a whole have remained quite stable. Furthermore, within each subgroup the increases were fairly uniform.

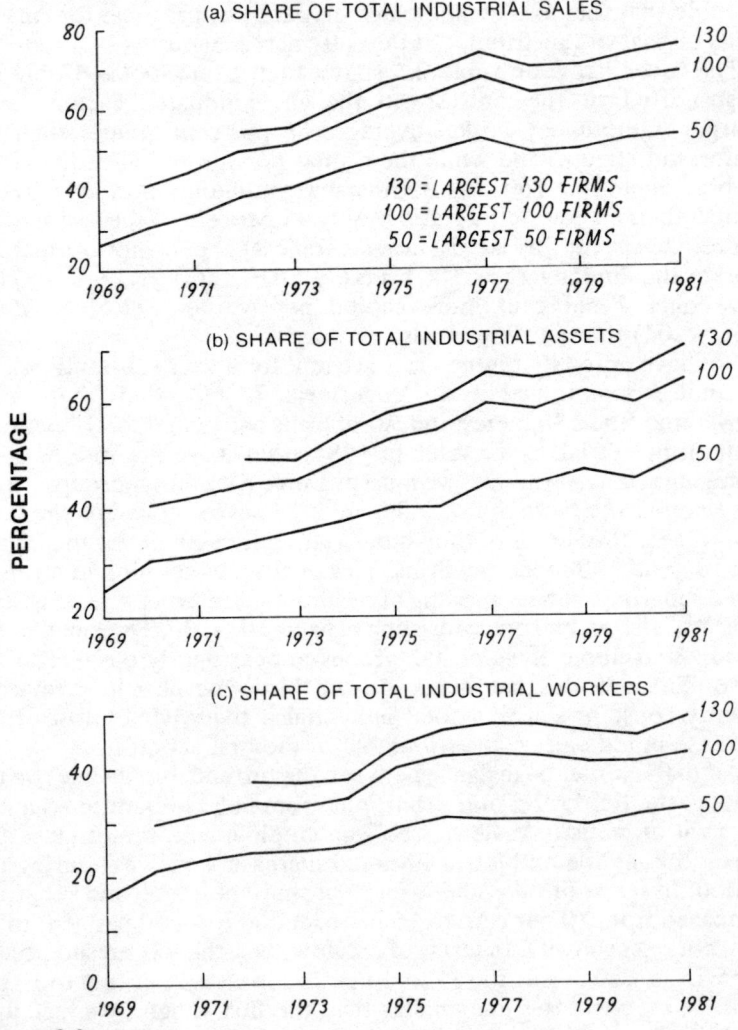

Figure 2.2

In the trade sector, changes over this period were less dramatic. Figure 2.3 shows that the top fifty firms' share of trade sector sales rose only from 34 per cent to 36 per cent, while their share of total sector assets rose from 27 per cent in 1969 to 38 per cent in 1981. Only in

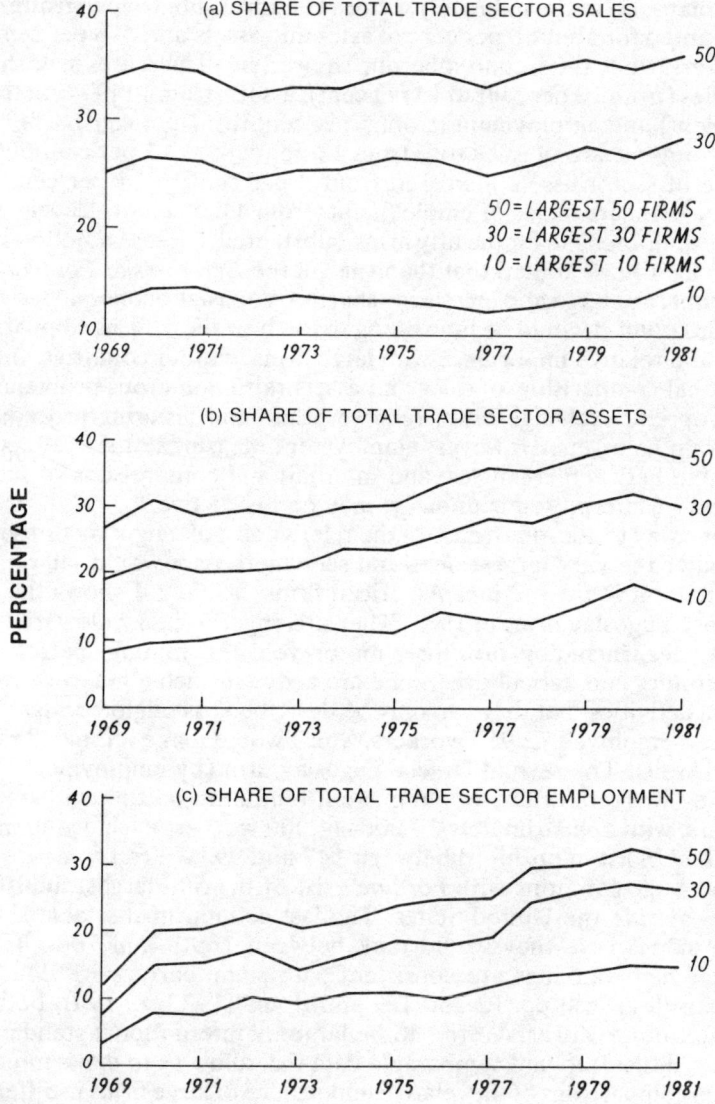

Figure 2.3

terms of employment has their relative importance increased substantially, from 12 per cent to 31 per cent, with much of this increase occurring in 1970 and 1978. If we divide the large firms into three subgroups (the first ten, the next twenty, and the last twenty), their relative importance in terms of total growth over the decade is much like that seen in the industrial sector. The third subgroup consistently accounted for about 8 per cent of sales and assets and 4–6 per cent of workers, while the second subgroup showed small increases in its share of sales (from 12 per cent to 13 per cent), assets (from 11 per cent to 14 per cent) and employment (from 5 per cent to 11 per cent). The first subgroup's share of sales rose from 13 per cent to 15 per cent but its share of sector assets increased from 8 per cent to 17 per cent. Its increased share of sector employment (from 4 per cent to 15 per cent) is the major reason for the fifty firms' substantial increase noted above.

So far I have argued that the firms on the *Ekonomska Politika* list account for a large and increasing share of Yugoslav economic activity. At this point it would be interesting to ask how these firms compare in size and relative importance with large firms in other countries. International comparisons of sales and assets raise numerous problems of appropriate exchange rates, relative prices and differing procedures for valuing assets. However, employment measures of size are comparable between countries, and international comparisons of sector shares, if interpreted cautiously, may be instructive.

One way to get some sense of the relative size of Yugoslav firms is to consider the very largest ones and see where they would fall on the *Fortune* '500' list of giant American firms. Table 2.4 shows the ten largest Yugoslav firms in 1981. They are engaged in a wide variety of industries, including furniture, motor vehicles, mining, petroleum, electronics and agriculture. Some are active in such a heterogeneous set of activities that they can only be described as conglomerates. The biggest employed 72,917 workers, which would make it rank 42nd on the US list. The second largest Yugoslav firm (by employment) had 48,687 workers, which would make it rank 88th on the US list. The others, with approximately 30,000–44,000 workers each, would rank on the US list in positions between 147 and 99. We can compare the same Yugoslav firms with *Fortune*'s list of the 500 largest industrial firms *outside* the United States. The last column of the table shows that in this case they would rank between 169th and 70th. These rather high rankings are consistent with some early work done by Rockwell (1968, pp. 12 and 15) and Pryor (1973, p. 194), both of whom found Yugoslav firms to be large by international standards.

It is difficult to find comparable data that allow us to make international comparisons of the relative importance of large firms in different countries. The major problem is that the industrial sector may be

Table 2.4 *Yugoslavia's Ten Largest Firms as Measured by Employment, 1981*

Firm	Number of workers	Rank (by employment) among Fortune's 500 largest US firms	Rank (by employment) among Fortune's 500 largest non-US firms
Šipad (wood products)	72,917	42	70
Crvena Zastava (motor vehicles)	48,687	88	99
Rudarsko Metalurški Kombinat Zenica (mining-metalurgy)	44,318	99	110
Energoinvest (conglomerate)	42,404	104	115
Makedonija (agroindustry)	41,085	109	121
Unis (conglomerate)	35,000	128	139
UPI (agroindustry)	34,019	132	144
INA (petroleum)	30,205	146	165
Poljoprivredni Kombinat Beograd (agroindustry)	30,016	146	168
ISKRA (electronics)	29,942	147	169

defined differently in different countries. In Yugoslavia it is very broadly defined to include mining, agriculture and fishing, forestry, and construction. Thus if, for example, construction is more or less concentrated than a more narrowly defined industrial sector, an international comparison would be biased.

We do have for some years separate data for Yugoslav industry and mining alone. These data are available only for more recent years and the number of giant firms included varies from year to year and is less than 100 in every case. Therefore, the study of changes over time, which constitutes the heart of this chapter, cannot be built on those data. However, they do indicate the approximate effect of using the wider definition. In 1981, ninety-six of the 140 largest firms were in the narrowly defined industry and mining sector. Those ninety-six accounted for 74 per cent of narrowly defined industrial sales, 63 per cent of value added, 70 per cent of assets and 50 per cent of employment (*Ekonomska Politika*, no. 1592, 4 October, 1982, p. 43). Adjusting for the use of ninety-six rather than 100 firms, it appears that the narrowly defined industrial sector is about 10 per cent more concentrated than the broadly defined one (see Table 2.5).

Table 2.5 *Aggregate Concentration in Several Industrialized Countries*

Country (year)	Largest 100 firms' share of industrial sector			
	Sales %	Value added %	Assets %	Employment %
Yugoslavia (1981)	69	55	64	43
Yugoslavia (1975)	61	47	54	40
Yugoslavia (1970)	41		41	30
Canada (1965)		44		
Great Britain (1968)		41		
Japan (1970)	29		50[a]	
Sweden (1963)		46		
United States (1972)	32	33	47	23
West Germany (1971)	52			17[b]

[a] Japan's asset share is for 1967.
[b] Germany's employment share is for 1961.

Source: Yugoslav data calculated from *Ekonomska Politika*, various issues. Other countries from Scherer (1980, pp. 47 and 50–2), except German employment figure from Pryor (1973, p. 183).

Despite the potential hazards discussed above, international comparisons may still be useful. Scherer (1970, pp. 40, 44 and 45; 1980, pp. 47 and 50–2) has collected what little data are available. In Table 2.5 I present his figures along with my results for Yugoslavia for three different years. Clearly, for all four of the size measures, the 100 largest Yugoslav firms account for a larger share of industrial activity than do the 100 largest firms in the other countries. In the sales and assets columns the Yugoslav figure for 1970 is not the highest, but by 1975 Yugoslavia had surpassed the countries for which comparable data are available.

Not shown in Table 2.5 are the following additional fragmentary comparisons of employment by large firms: in France the largest twenty-five firms accounted for 16 per cent of industrial employment, while the corresponding Yugoslav figure is 21 per cent; in Japan the largest thirty-seven firms employed 11 per cent of the industrial labor force, as compared with 26 per cent for the same number of firms in

Yugoslavia; in the UK, 29 per cent of the industrial labor force were employed by the fifty-three largest firms vs. 32 per cent in Yugoslavia. Again the Yugoslav figures are all higher than comparable numbers for other countries. These data for France, Japan and the UK are taken from Scherer (1970, pp. 40, 44 and 45) and are for 1963, while the Yugoslav data are for 1981. There may be some question about the appropriateness of comparing Yugoslav concentration figures for 1981 with figures for other countries for the early 1960s. Indeed, earlier Yugoslav data would give different results. But Pryor (1973, p. 184) claims that in other countries 'the share accounted for by the largest enterprises does not show a general pattern of increase', while in Yugoslavia the increasing trend is unmistakable. The very point to be made here is that by the mid-1970s Yugoslavia had exceeded the level of aggregate concentration characteristic of developed capitalist countries in the early 1960s. Whether there have been significant changes in the capitalist countries since then is a matter of some debate, but not of great importance here. Of course, we should keep in mind that the total size of the Yugoslav economy is smaller than those it is being compared with. If Pryor was correct in suggesting a negative relationship between the size of the domestic market and the degree of concentration, then we might expect the share of the giants to decline as the Yugoslav economy grows. However, these data do not support that hypothesis.

Some Different Empirical Evidence

The empirical evidence presented so far was calculated from the *Ekonomska Politika* lists of large firms. We turn now to a different source of information about the size of economic units in the Yugoslav economy, the *Statistical Yearbook*. This source conveys an entirely different picture of the changes that occurred in Yugoslav industrial structure during the 1970s. Instead of the increasing importance of large firms, it shows the growing significance of small units. The reason for the difference is that they are measuring different phenomena. *Ekonomska Politika* has consistently dealt with what is regarded in the business world as an enterprise or firm. The term enterprise (*preduzeće*) is officially out of favor, but the same concept, now usually called work organization (*radna organizacija*), is still widely regarded as a meaningful economic unit and as appropriate for statistical analysis, despite the emphasis that the constitutional amendments of 1971, the new Constitution of 1974 and the Law on Associated Labor of 1976 have placed on the autonomy of the divisions of enterprises. The Federal Statistical Institute, on the other hand, has shifted its focus

Table 2.6 Total Number of Economic Units

	1969	1970	1971	1972	1973	1974	1975	1976	1977	1978	1979	1980
Industrial sector[a]	2,435	2,374	2,398	2,773	3,217	4,100	6,495	7,320	7,731	8,414	8,984	9,306
Trade sector[b]	3,132	2,901	2,968	3,683	3,689	3,881	5,423	5,150	5,269	5,661	5,842	5,998
Total social sector	11,817	11,100	11,102	12,583	13,119	14,933	21,414	22,109	22,929	24,949	26,408	27,400

[a] Includes mining.
[b] Includes catering and tourism.

Source: Savezni Zavod za Statistiku, *Statistički Godišnjak Jugoslavije* for the years 1971–82. In each yearbook there is a section titled 'Opšti pregled privrednih delatnosti' from which these data are taken.

Table 2.7 Relative Significance of Industrial Sector Economic Units with Over 1,000 Workers

Share of total industrial	1969 %	1970 %	1971 %	1972 %	1973 %	1974 %	1975 %	1976 %	1977 %	1978 %	1979 %	1980 %
Sales	63	64	65	63	58	50	24	21	17	15	13	14
Assets	64	63	62	57	52	42	24	19	16	15	14	14
Employment	60	61	63	61	57	46	22	19	16	14	12	11

Source: Calculated from data on size distributions in Savezni Zavod za Statistiku, *Statistički Bilten*, Nos 695, 734, 769, 825, 883, 955, 1025 and 1080 and *Statistički Godišnjak Jugoslavije* 1979, p. 259; 1980, p. 259; 1981, p. 260; 1982, p. 261.

onto the subunits of enterprises. Beginning with 1972 it treated as separate statistical units those enterprise divisions that had the status of a legal person, and beginning in 1973 its 'number of units' refers to the basic organizations of associated labor, or BOALs, which is the official term for the divisions of enterprises. Only in cases where an enterprise is not structured as a collection of BOALs does the Statistical Institute count the entire enterprise as a single statistical unit.[3]

Table 2.6 shows changes during this period in the number of divisions. In the industrial sector (which is defined more narrowly here than in the *Ekonomska Politika* data), the number nearly quadrupled, after having held fairly constant between 2,350 and 2,800 from 1960 to 1972. In the trade sector, the number of units nearly doubled. For the entire social sector, the number more than doubled. Note that a substantial increase in the number of divisions in no way conflicts with the implication of the *Ekonomska Politika* data that large firms are playing an increasingly significant role in the economy. What we see in Table 2.6 is not an explosion in the number of firms, as that word is normally used by both Yugoslav and western businessmen. Rather, what is happening is an active implementation of the process of divisionalization that was mandated by the various legal changes of the 1970s. There is no reason that this process cannot occur simultaneously with the increasing relative importance of large firms. The two trends are logically quite compatible.

One aspect of these changes has been a decrease in the number of units in the largest two size categories (those with over 1,000 workers). Data on the aggregate relative weight of these units are available for the industrial sector, but not for the trade sector or for the entire social sector. Table 2.7 presents aggregate sales, assets and employment data for these units. The data are given as percentages of the total industrial sector. Whether we look at sales, assets or employment, units with over 1,000 workers account for a sharply declining share of total industrial activity. The downturn began in 1972 or 1973 and by 1980 their share was less than a quarter of what it had been in 1969.

Figure 2.4 shows, for selected years, size distributions for the economic units in the *Statistical Yearbook* data. It is quite clear that as the number of units increased, their relative dispersion decreased; that is, there is relatively less inequality of size. The largest increases in numbers of units were in size categories C–F. Because of the way the Statistical Institute defines the size categories, these units are quite small (30–500 workers).

Hart and Prais (1956, p. 151) have suggested that reduced variance of size distributions implies more competitiveness, but what is more important here is the relationship between divisions. This is a matter of conduct, which is much harder to measure than the structural

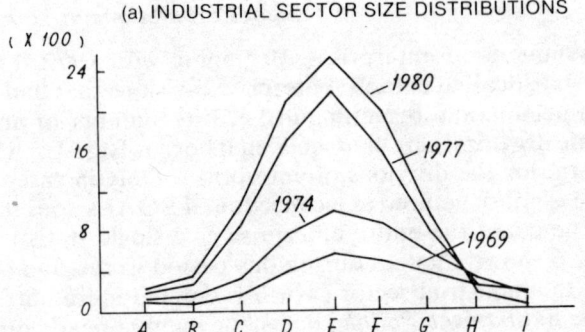
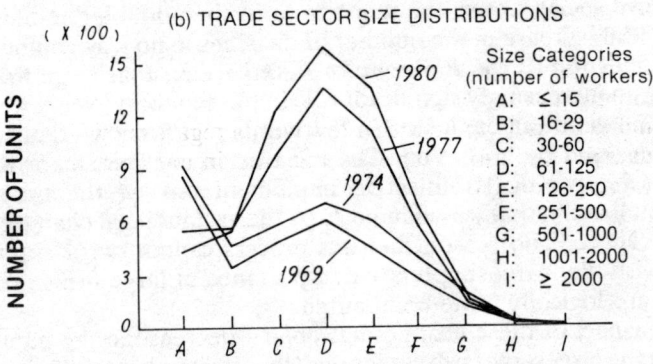
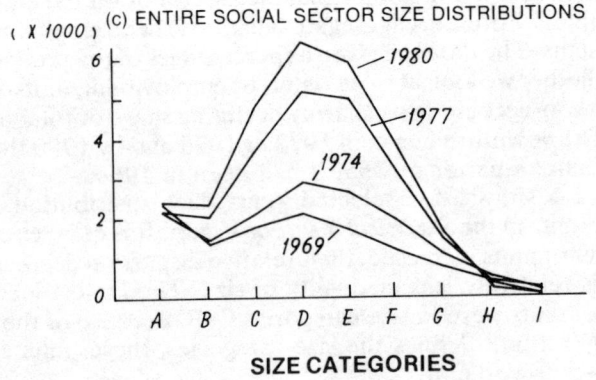

Figure 2.4

questions examined in this chapter. There is, however, some evidence to suggest that one form of collusion, market sharing, has not yet been carried very far. If agreements to divide up markets by product (e.g. 'I'll produce refrigerators and you make dishwashers') were common, we would expect to see a decline over time in the number of producers of each product. Data are available on the number of producers for each of several hundred specific industrial products (e.g. TV sets, small electric motors, copper tubing, fish nets, etc.). There are 344 products that were identically defined in 1969 and 1980 (Savezni Zavod za Statistiku, 1970, 1981). Of those, exactly half (172) were produced by more manufacturers at the end of the period than at the beginning. Just over a quarter of them (95) were made by fewer competitors in 1980, and the remainder (77) had the same number of producers in 1969 and 1980.[4] These are figures one would expect from a normally dynamic market economy. Certainly there is no evidence of a general decline in the number of competitors.

I conclude this chapter with a few words regarding why these structural changes are occurring. The increase in numbers of divisions is clearly a response to political decisions incorporated into major pieces of legislation adopted during the 1970s. Thus a full explanation requires an analysis of political forces rather than of the logic of the theory of the labor-managed firm. The other major change – the increasing relative importance of large firms – is at least partly explained by the economic benefits that accrue to those workers whose firms become large. When a group of divisions merge to form a large enterprise they not only begin to acquire some control over the price of their product, but they also improve their access to capital. Perhaps if the Yugoslav banking system were better able to estimate future profits of borrowers (or if it were replaced by a financing scheme proposed in Vanek, 1977), then this would not be the case. But at present in Yugoslavia the fact is that large firms do have easier access to capital, and this is likely to be a powerful incentive for the growth of large firms. An even more important reason for divisions jointly to constitute an enterprise is that this reduces the cost of transactions among them. This concept is the focus of chapter 4.

Summary

Because the efficiency of the Yugoslav economy depends in part on the functioning of a market mechanism, the size of firms is of considerable importance. If firms are large and/or very unequal in size then some will have inappropriate advantages over their competitors.

Furthermore, the distribution of decision-making power will be more unequal than is desired in a socialist country.

The substantiation or refutation of Vanek's predictions about firm size depends entirely on which body of data we point to. If we think in terms of the traditional firm, that is, a cohesive body that generally acts as a single unit or as a collection of units that act collusively, then it is the *Ekonomska Politika* data that seem appropriate. In that case the behavior of the Yugoslav economy does not support Vanek's analysis. There have developed what one might reasonably call 'inordinate concentrations of industrial power', and conglomerates are considerably easier to find than the apocalyptic beast with seven heads and ten horns. The danger of gigantism is very real, and competitive conditions could be said to be deteriorating as the discrepancy in size between the largest firms and the others increases. An impetus to grow and to control a sizable portion of the market is apparent.

On the other hand, if we think in terms of a different economic unit, the division, which in recent years has increased its importance and autonomy, then it is the Statistical Institute's data that we should rely on. In this case the behavior of the Yugoslav economic system does indeed support Vanek's predictions. Over the thirteen years 1969–81 there has been a sharp increase in the number of actors and a decrease in the variance of their size distribution. The very strong movement toward economic units of under 500 workers, each with homogeneous activities, is undeniable.

It is impossible to say that one of these is the *correct* way to analyze structural changes in the Yugoslav economy, so we should consider for each the likely implications for the viability of competition in Yugoslavia. If we focus our attention on the *Ekonomska Politika* data it is important to remember that the increasing discrepancy in size is between the giants *taken as a group* and the rest of the economy. *Within* the group of giants (which in 1981 accounted for 49 per cent of employment in the industrial sector and 31 per cent in the trade sector) relative shares have remained fairly stable. Competition within this large segment of the economy shows no sign of lessening over time. If we focus on the Statistical Institute data on divisions, the prospects for effective competition would seem to be even more promising. But in this case what is most important for the effectiveness of competition is the nature of these corporate giants. The question is, what is the relationship among the constituent components of the firm?

Competition among divisions within a single firm is sometimes quite keen. The autonomy and independence of divisions, including the fact that workers' incomes depend largely on their own division's performance, suggest some degree of competition. Even after a merger there is the possibility of continued competition, as when a Slovenian food processor merged with a chain of supermarkets to take 29th place on the list of giants, or when three makers of liquor and confections merged to take 42nd place. Since these supermarkets are not forced to buy from their sister division, and the divisions making various brands of cognac do continue to try to outsell one another, the economic discipline of competition need not significantly diminish. There is evidence of competition among the divisions of the Zagreb brewery. On the other hand, to the extent that divisions within enterprises divide up markets and fix prices, the vigor of competition among them, and hence the efficiency of the market mechanism, is lessened.

Notes

1 This principle was first shown by Ward (1958), and later by Domar (1966). Numerous others have acknowledged and modified it. The following summary is based on Vanek's *General Theory* (1970), especially chapters 2 and 6.
2 For a number of reasons, the 1968 data are not useful for comparisons over time. In subsequent years the number of industrial sector firms listed was: 53 in 1969; 100 in 1970 and 1971; 130 for 1972–77; and 140 after 1977. The number of trade sector firms is 50 up to 1977 and 60 thereafter. The industrial sector is defined very broadly and includes large-scale agriculture, forestry and construction as well as manufacturing and mining. The trade sector includes tourism and catering (mainly hotels) as well as wholesale, retail and foreign trade.
3 Just when the Statistical Institute started to count divisions instead of enterprises is not entirely clear. Until 1972, data on number of enterprises were published in *Statistički Godišnjak Jugoslavije* (*Statistical Yearbook of Yugoslavia*) under the column heading 'Ukupan broj privrednih organizacija' (total number of economic organizations). Beginning with the data for 1972 (which appeared in the 1974 *Yearbook*), the column heading was 'Broj jedinica' (number of units), and a footnote specified that what was being counted was OOURs (that is, BOALs) and those OURs (work organizations or enterprises) that were not broken up into OOURs. After the 1976 data (that is, the 1978 *Yearbook*), the footnote was dropped.

However, the following paragraph, taken from *Statistički Bilten*, No. 1086, titled 'Industrija 1977' ('Clarifications and notes', pp. 7 and 8), suggests that the change was several years later. In the hope that it may be of some help to other researchers, I have translated the entire paragraph:

> *Radna organizacija* was the basic statistical unit up to 1974. All data related to the organization as a whole, without regard to whether some of it had territorially separate units [*pogone*] or a large number of different activities. . . . Beginning with 1975 the statistical system was adapted to the forms of associated labor, and in place of *radna organizacija* (previously *preduzeće*) [i.e. enterprise], the OOUR became the basic statistical unit [*jedinica*]. However, although for 1975 the data were collected by OOUR, in order to be comparable with data for earlier years, they have in processing been reduced to the level of the former *radne organizacije*. Data for 1976 and 1977 are processed according to the activities of the OOUR and not according to the activities of the *radne organizacije*.
>
> It should be kept in mind that during these years most enterprises were in the process of restructuring themselves in order to meet the requirements of the new laws, which

encouraged increased divisionalization. Thus, during the middle years of the 1970s, both the counting method and the items being counted were in a process of change.

4 Detailed examination of changes during sub-periods shows no surprising patterns. Most products that had an increased number of producers over the whole period had increases in the sub-periods (only fifteen of them had decreases 1969–77 and only sixteen had decreases 1977–80). Of those that had decreases overall, most decreased in the sub-periods (only twenty-three showed an increase in one of the sub-periods). Seventy-two products showed down–up or up–down behavior in different sub-periods.

3 The Theory of Transfer Prices

Transfer prices are the prices charged when one division of a firm sells a product or service to another division of the same firm. If the firm were run by a central administration, then transfer prices would serve merely an accounting function or as a device for distributing income. However, since Yugoslav enterprises consist of autonomous divisions, transfer prices affect input and output decisions and hence the overall efficiency of the firm.

This chapter is divided into two sections. The first examines the inefficient allocation of labor that can result from decentralization within a labor-managed enterprise, and shows that this inefficiency can be eliminated by the use of proper transfer prices. The second section deals with the allocation of non-labor inputs in the labor-managed firm. It shows that if transfer prices are not optimal, the resulting efficiency loss will be less, *ceteris paribus*, than in a capitalist firm.

It should be made clear at the beginning that this chapter focuses on marginal decisions. That is, it deals with the efficient use of existing facilities. The question of whether or not to establish a new division or to abandon an existing one demands consideration of total, as well as marginal, cost and revenue.

Allocation of Labor

It is well known that a labor-managed economy may suffer from immobility of labor between firms where marginal productivity is high and those where it is low. It is not, however, widely recognized that this same inefficiency can occur with regard to the allocation of labor within a decentralized firm.

This is most easily seen in the simple case where labor is the only variable input. Consider an enterprise with two divisions, each of which sets its output level so as to maximize profit per worker or, to use Domar's (1966) term, dividend. Using the conventional model[1] we can say that division A seeks to maximize

$$D_A = (Q_A P_A - R_A)/L_A,$$

where D_A is the dividend, or profit per worker, earned in division A,
Q_A is the output of division A (and is a function of L_A),
P_A is the price of division A's product (and is assumed fixed),
R_A is the cost of other inputs (which are fixed), and
L_A is the number of workers in division A.

Similarly, division B chooses its labor input so as to maximize D_B, which is defined analogously. Assuming decreasing marginal productivity of labor, each division will hire labor up to the point where the value of its marginal product falls to the dividend in that division; further workers will not be hired because they would contribute less to division income than they would take as their share of profits and thus they would dilute the earnings of the others.

If the divisions produce different products, have different capital endowments and/or employ different technologies, it is obviously quite possible that they may have different dividend curves. Figure 3.1 shows the dividend and value of the marginal product of labor (VMP) curves for both divisions (drawn back to back). When division A hires a_1 workers, thus maximizing their dividend, the value of the marginal product of labor is less than in division B, which chooses to hire b_1 workers. In order to correct this inefficiency, workers would have to be shifted from division A to division B until the value of the marginal product of labor is equal in the two divisions. In Figure 3.1 this would occur when $a_1 - a_2 \,(= b_2 - b_1)$ workers are shifted.

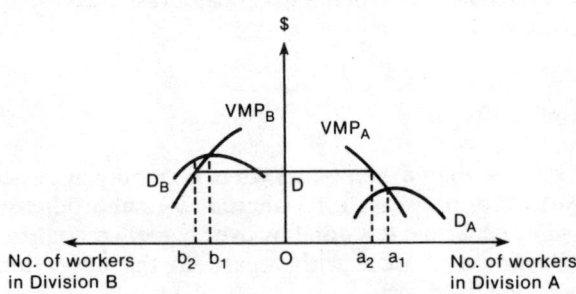

Figure 3.1

However, division B will not be willing to take on additional workers, because that would push it beyond its optimal labor input. Nor would the workers remaining in division A want reduced labor input in their division, since that would reduce their dividend. Thus, if each division is left to maximize its own profit per worker, the firm as a

The Theory of Transfer Prices 49

whole will not be using labor efficiently and hence will not be maximizing overall profit per worker. Since there is no central office of the enterprise with authority to order one division to accept additional workers from another division, it seems that the inefficiency will persist.

The Internal Sale of Services

There is, however, a way other than outright commands from a central office in which something equivalent to the reallocation of workers between divisions can be achieved: division A can undertake to sell some service to division B. This does not mean that division A will explicitly contract to supply a given number of man-hours of labor; rather, workers who continue to be members of (i.e. paid by and share in the profits of) division A are assigned to perform specific tasks for division B (for example, bookkeeping or cleaning services, which in Yugoslav firms often are provided by a separate division). Division B then pays division A (not the workers) directly for the services provided. Now, hiring workers without giving them a full share in profits and management conflicts with the basic principles of the Yugoslav economy. However, buying a service at a fixed price from another firm or division, as division B is doing here, does not violate those principles, although it amounts to the same thing. Thus the internal sale of services reallocates labor legitimately. The tasks that are to be performed must be clearly identified and such that it is possible to calculate the equivalent number of man-days involved. Division B must be able to calculate the value to itself of the service.

Division A now seeks to maximize

$$D^*_A = (Q_A P_A + ST - R_A)/L_A,$$

where Q_A, P_A, R_A and L_A are defined as for D_A, S is the amount (measured in number of workers) of the service sold by A, and T is the price of the service (per unit of service equivalent to one worker).

In the short run, the number of members of division A (i.e. L_A) is fixed, and the important decision is how many of its workers division A wants to assign to performing services to be sold to division B. Differentiating D^*_A with respect to S and setting equal to zero, we get

$$\frac{dD^*_A}{dS} = \frac{d}{dS}\left(\frac{Q_A P_A}{L_A} + \frac{ST}{L_A} - \frac{R_A}{L_A}\right) = 0,$$

$$(1/L_A)(-VMP_A + T - 0) = 0,$$

$$VMP_A = T.$$

That is, division A's dividend is maximized when the number of interdivisional workers (those assigned to performing services for division B) is such that the value of the marginal product of labor of regular workers in division A (those not assigned to services to be sold to division B) equals the price of the intermediate service. This is hardly surprising since, when we hold L_A fixed, division A is maximizing total profit, as well as profit per worker.

Similarly, division B seeks to maximize

$$D^*_B = (Q_B P_B - ST - R_B)/L_B.$$

Maximization requires

$$\frac{dD^*_B}{dS} = \frac{d}{dS}\left(\frac{Q_B P_B}{L_B} - \frac{ST}{L_B} - \frac{R_B}{L_B}\right) = 0,$$

$$(1/L_B)(VMP_B - T - 0) = 0,$$

$$VMP_B = T.$$

Hence, division B maximizes its own dividend when the quantity it purchases of the intermediate service is such that the value of the marginal product of labor (of those working for division B, regardless of which division they are members of) equals the price of the service. Thus, both divisions equate the value of the marginal product of labor to a common value T, thereby ensuring that the value of the marginal product of labor is the same in the two divisions.

In the long run, the sum of the number of regular workers in division A (denoted below by $W = L_A - S$) plus the number of interdivisional workers (denoted below, as above, by S) is not constrained to equal a fixed labor force, L_A. Given time to adjust its membership, division A's dividend function becomes

$$D^*_A = (Q_A P_A + ST - R_A)/(W + S),$$

where $Q_A, P_A, R_A,$ and T are defined as before except that Q_A is now a function of W. Differentiating D^*_A with respect to W and setting equal to zero, we get

$$\frac{\partial D^*_A}{\partial W^*_A} = \frac{\partial}{\partial W}\left(\frac{Q_A P_A}{W+S} + \frac{ST}{W+S} - \frac{R_A}{W+S}\right) = 0$$

$$\frac{VMP_A(W+S) - Q_A P_A - ST + R_A}{(W+S)^2} = 0,$$

$$VMP_A = \frac{Q_A P_A + ST - R_A}{W + S}.$$

That is, in the long run division A will maximize its dividend by following the same rule it follows when the internal sale of services is not considered: hire regular workers up to the point where the value of their marginal product falls to the dividend being earned.

At the same time, the division must choose the quantity of interdivisional workers. Differentiating D^*_A with respect to S, we get

$$\frac{\partial D^*_A}{\partial S} = \frac{\partial}{\partial S}\left(\frac{Q_A P_A}{W + S} + \frac{ST}{W + S} - \frac{R_A}{W + S}\right)$$

$$= -\frac{Q_A P_A}{(W + S)^2} + \frac{T[(W + S) - S]}{(W + S)^2} + \frac{R_A}{(W + S)^2}$$

$$= \frac{T - (Q_A P_A - R_A)/W}{(W + S)^2/W}.$$

The right-hand term in the numerator of the fraction is the dividend that would be earned by regular workers if there were no interdivisional sale of services. If T (the price of the service) is greater than that dividend, then the derivative of D^*_A with respect to S will be positive, and the division's dividend will increase as S increases. Since second- and higher-order derivatives all equal zero, the dividend will increase without limit as S increases. That is, they will sell as much of the service as division B is willing to buy. If T is less than the dividend generated by regular workers, the derivative will be negative and the division will set S equal to zero, i.e. not sell the service at all.

It is interesting to notice that since the sale of an intermediate service raises the dividend in both divisions, initiation of such sales tends to reduce the number of regular workers in division A and the number of members of division B. This results from the rule that each division will hire members up to the point where the value of their marginal product equals the dividend.

Setting the Transfer Price

The provision of a service by division A to division B not only improves the overall efficiency of the firm, but benefits both divisions; some of the division A members are earning more than what would have been their marginal product had they not provided services to the other division, and division B is getting work done at a price that is (for the intramarginal workers) less than its value to the division. There is, therefore, no need for a central office to impose this arrangement. The initiative might, of course, come from some central body, but it might also come from either of the divisions. Similarly, in setting a transfer price the center might facilitate reaching an agreement, but it is not absolutely needed since representatives of the two divisions could be expected to settle on a price. In the short run (when the membership of each division is fixed), the correct price from the point of view of the whole firm is OD in Figure 3.1: this is the price that will induce the sale of a quantity of the service equivalent to $a_1 - a_2 \ (= b_2 - b_1)$ workers. Since OD is the only transfer price at which the quantity offered for sale by division A equals the quantity demanded by division B, there should be no problem in agreeing on the transfer price.

In the long run more calculations are needed. While transfer price OD will equalize the value of the marginal product of labor in the two divisions, it is not necessarily true that the size of the total labor force is optimal for the whole firm. The overall firm dividend (which is the weighted average of the dividends of the divisions) may be either greater or smaller than OD. If the firm's dividend is less than OD, the firm will benefit from hiring more workers because they will contribute more to revenue than they will take out as profit share. More workers will be hired if the transfer price is lowered (assuming division A can be convinced to accept a lower transfer price). Division B will then be willing to purchase more of the intermediate service, while division A, given time to adjust its total membership, will supply as much as B is willing to buy. Sale of the service continues to equalize productivity between the two divisions. At the optimal total labor input the firm's dividend will equal the firm's value of the marginal product, and the transfer price will equal both. If, on the other hand, when labor is first reallocated between divisions, the firm's dividend is larger than the marginal productivity OD, then the firm is employing too much labor; the transfer price should be raised, thus reducing B's willingness to buy the intermediate service (and hence reducing, in the long run, membership in A), and raising the marginal productivity of labor in both divisions. In this case division B must be convinced to pay a higher transfer price.

Allocation of Non-labor Inputs

Ward (1967, p. 195) and Vanek (1970, pp. 49–52) have shown that the labor-managed firm's demand for non-labor inputs is, in comparable circumstances, the same as the capitalist firm's. Therefore, in analyzing the role of transfer prices in the allocation of non-labor inputs, we can draw on established theory. Consider a capitalist firm that has two divisions, one that produces an intermediate good and

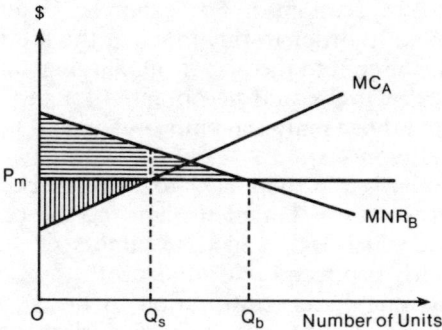

Figure 3.2

another that uses it. Figure 3.2 shows division A's marginal cost (MC_A) of producing intermediate good A and also division B's marginal net revenue (MNR_B). MNR_B is the additional revenue division B earns from each extra unit of its output minus all additional costs of producing that extra unit except the cost of the intermediate product that it is buying from division A. The horizontal axis has to be measured in two different units: units of the intermediate product A, and units equal to the quantity of B that can be produced from each unit of A (thus a fixed input coefficient is assumed).[2] If we assume that costs in both divisions are increasing (at least in the relevant range), the MC_A slopes upward and MNR_B slopes downward. The usual marginal revenue curve for division B is not drawn. If B's product is sold in a perfectly competitive market, the marginal revenue curve will be horizontal; otherwise it will slope downward. In either case MNR_B will slope downward, although it need not always be a straight line.

Hirshleifer (1956, 1957) has shown that if there exists a competitive external market for the intermediate good, then the firm should set its transfer price, P_m, equal to the external price. Division A will then choose to produce and sell quantity Q_s, while division B will operate at point Q_b. Division B buys quantity Q_s from division A plus it buys the difference between Q_s and Q_b on the open market. Notice that if some central office were to force division A to provide more of division B's needs, the firm as a whole would be wasting resources since its cost for the extra units of the intermediate good would be greater than necessary.

It is, of course, possible that the price on external markets will be above the intersection of MC_A and MNR_B. In that case, division B will buy less than the total output of division A and the rest will be sold outside the firm. Again, any transfer price not equal to P_m will encourage division behavior that is wasteful from the point of view of the firm as a whole (and, if market prices are true scarcity prices, from the point of view of the entire economy). For example, if division B were persuaded to expand in order to buy more of the intermediate good produced by A, the benefit to the firm from marginal units of A would be less than the price that could be obtained for those units on the outside market (and those marginal units of A would be socially more valuable in alternative uses).

Another possibility is that there is no external market for the intermediate good. In this case, Hirshleifer shows, the optimal transfer price is that price at which MC_A and MNR_B intersect. At that price the intermediate good is produced and used up to the point where the value of its inputs equals its contribution to the value of the final output. The firm is then neither a supplier nor a demander on external markets.

In the labor-managed firm, just as in a capitalist firm, a non-labor input is used up to the point where the value of its marginal product equals price. That is, the demand curve for the intermediate good will reflect its marginal net revenue to the buying division. Similarly, there is a supply curve for the intermediate product that reflects division A's costs (measured at the 'full wage' earned by labor, which includes a share of profit or loss). As in the capitalist case, efficiency requires that if an external competitive market exists for the intermediate good, the transfer price should equal the market price. If no external market exists (or if the external market is not competitive), the optimal transfer price is determined by the intersection of the internal supply and demand curves.

Measuring the Efficiency Loss
Let us look more carefully at the case where the transfer price is set at some level other than the optimal price P_m. P_m could be below, at or above the intersection of MC_A and MNR_B; furthermore, a non-optimal transfer price may be above or below P_m. But in order to be brief, I examine here only the case shown in Figure 3.3. Although the geometry would be slightly different, the conclusions apply to all possibilities.

Suppose the selling division succeeds in establishing a transfer price that is higher than P_m, such as P_t as shown in Figure 3.3. Suppose also that the buying division is allowed to buy the intermediate good from outside suppliers only if its needs exceed its sister division's output. Then quantity Q'_s is produced and sold internally, and the profits of the selling division (as shown by the vertically shaded areas in Figures 3.2 and 3.3) increase, while the profits of the buying division (as shown by the horizontally shaded areas) decrease.[3] It is important to notice that this is not just a matter of one division gaining what another has lost: the increase in the selling division's profit is less than the decrease

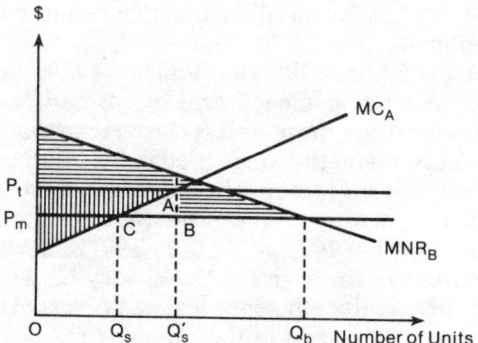

Figure 3.3

in the buying division's profit, the difference being measured by the area of triangle ABC. This net reduction in overall enterprise profit is the result of the non-optimal output decisions that are made when the transfer price is not an accurate measure of alternatives. That is, the artificially high transfer price encourages the firm to produce more of the intermediate good than it should. The selling division benefits, but the firm as a whole (and the society) suffers from the irrational use of resources.[4]

Determinants of the Size of the Efficiency Loss

An important question is whether the efficiency loss from non-optimal transfer prices is the same in the labor-managed enterprise as in the capitalist enterprise. The answer hinges on the elasticities of the marginal cost and marginal revenue curves. They obviously have an important effect on the efficiency loss that results when the transfer price deviates from its optimal level. In Figure 3.3 the height of the triangle ABC is equal to the difference between the optimal price P_m and the actual transfer price P_t. The length of the base of the triangle is determined by the slope of MC_A. For a given price discrepancy between optimal and actual transfer prices, the more inelastic the marginal cost curve (i.e. the producing division's supply curve for the intermediate good), the smaller the efficiency loss.

There are a number of possible relationships among P_m, P_t and the intersection of MC_A and MNR_B other than that shown in Figure 3.3; but in every case the size of the efficiency loss depends in part on the size of a triangle whose height equals the price discrepancy and whose base decreases with decreases in the elasticity of either the supply curve of the producing division or the demand curve of the buying division. This is intuitively quite plausible: the less responsive the buyer and seller are to price (that is, the less elastic their demand and supply curves), the less the misallocation that results when the transfer price is not optimal.

Both Ward (1967, p. 198) and Vanek (1970, pp. 49–52) have shown that in the labor-managed firm the demand curve for a non-labor input may be either more or less elastic than that in the capitalist twin. Hence we cannot on that basis predict the relative size of triangle ABC. However, it is well known that the supply curve of the labor-managed firm is normally more inelastic than the supply curve of the capitalist twin (Ward, 1967, pp. 190–1, 197–8, 200; Vanek, 1970, pp. 45–6). Therefore, for a given discrepancy between optimal and actual transfer prices, the efficiency loss can be expected to be less in the labor-managed case than in the capitalist case.

Summary

Chapter 1 described the internal structure of self-managed corporations in Yugoslavia and chapter 2 showed that many of them are quite large. In those chapters I argued that transfer prices are more than a device for distributing income, that they do affect the quantity of goods and services produced by divisions. Chapter 3 shows a simple principle concerning the relationship among the divisions within a firm: transfer prices can have a significant effect on the efficiency of the use of resources by the enterprise. To the extent that transfer prices for services equate internal supply and demand for those services, their use contributes to the efficient allocation of labor within the firm. For goods, efficiency requires that transfer prices equal the prices on external markets, if those markets are competitive; otherwise, they should equal the marginal cost of the supplier division.

Thus, prices can play the same role within the firm that they play in other situations: they convey information that is useful in coordinating the activities of independent economic units. Of course, this idea is not unique to socialist corporations. This possibility has long been recognized for large capitalist firms (Whinston, 1964). In multinational corporations, prices can be used either as signals to improve resource allocation or as a means of intentionally shuffling profit between countries so as to minimize taxes (Booth and Jensen, 1977; Rugman, 1979; Feld, 1982). In chapter 7 I shall argue that the 'associations' being created in other socialist countries are in many respects like divisionalized firms. Hence this analysis of transfer prices can be applied there too. In the extreme case an entire economy can be viewed as a divisionalized firm.

Notes

1 This formulation of the objective of the labor-managed firm is used by Ward (1958), Domar (1966), Vanek (1970) and others. Vanek shows that it is equally appropriate, and that most of its implications are equally valid, when labor is one of several variable inputs.
2 The assumption of a fixed input coefficient is necessary only for the graphical analysis. While the analysis is more difficult without this assumption, the conclusions remain valid.
3 Strictly speaking, the area above the marginal cost curve and the area under the marginal net revenue curve do not measure profit but rather producer's surplus and buyer's surplus, respectively. However, since the analysis deals only with marginal adjustments, and not with decisions of whether to abandon a division, fixed costs can be ignored and these areas referred to as profit.
4 Solomons (1965, Appendix to chapter VI) points out that triangle ABC represents the net reduction in firm profit. He does not, however, discuss it in terms of efficiency loss.

4 Efficiency of Divisionalized Corporations

Introduction

In industrial organization literature, an assumption is sometimes made that new institutional forms are always more efficient than those they replace; indeed, it has been argued that we can learn what is efficient by watching what evolves.[1] Thus, it is generally believed that the divisionalization of corporations in capitalist countries, mentioned at the end of chapter 1, is a consequence of successful experimentation. Similarly, one would assume that the parallel process in socialist countries, to be discussed in chapter 7, probably resulted from expectations of improved productivity. But it should be made explicit that changes in organizational structure may be influenced by ideology as well as by narrow views about productive efficiency. Certainly in Yugoslavia the organizational structure of corporations results not from an unrestricted search for efficiency, but from decisions based at least in part on political ideology and expediency. Therefore, we must carefully examine that structure and analyze its likely implications.

A fundamental principle underlying the philosophy of the entire Yugoslav economic system is that wherever possible small work units are to be organized as separate, independent entities. As shown in chapter 1, this principle goes beyond the independence of enterprises from central control, and establishes the independence of divisions within the enterprise. Within the firm, a modified market mechanism is to be used rather than a command hierarchy. Even planning is to be done by joint decision among equals.

In this chapter I consider whether the Yugoslav divisionalization of firms is costly in terms of economic efficiency. One might claim that even if this organizational structure were inefficient in a narrow sense, the greater job satisfaction and reduced alienation of workers would more than compensate in terms of the effect on quantity or quality of goods produced. For example, Blumberg (1968) and others (Braverman, 1974) argue that worker participation leads to increased work satisfaction and hence higher output; Steinherr (1977) shows that some degree of profit sharing and participation is optimal and will improve the net productivity of the firm; and Tyson (1979) claims that decentralization within the labor-managed firm increases worker communication and team spirit and thus enhances the incentive effects of income sharing. Alternatively, one might argue that quantity of production is not important, that a system that gives workers a greater role in controlling their workplace is superior (perhaps even, in a broader sense, more efficient) *regardless* of the effect on output. Ironically, it may be that the divisionalization (some would call it fragmentation) of the Yugoslav firm may facilitate its very opposite: by breaking the firm up into pieces small enough to allow meaningful worker control, the Yugoslav system reduces the alienation that is an obstacle to worker solidarity. At the end of his study of the sociology of industrial democracy, Blumberg concludes (1968, p. 234) that 'genuine workers' management, then, tends to be an *integrative force* which . . . [may] offset the technological splintering and fragmentation which has been imposed upon the factory worker since the beginning of the industrial revolution'.

Such arguments cannot be dismissed lightly, but they are not the subject of this book. Furthermore, we want to know whether defenders of the Yugoslav system need to fall back on such arguments. That is, does the ideologically determined structure have a serious negative effect on efficiency? The main question is whether the divisionalization of enterprises reduces efficiency in the narrow sense by defeating the very purpose of creating firms.

In order to answer this question, it is necessary to consider why firms exist at all. This leads into an examination of the nature of the relationship among Yugoslav divisions. Whereas a major point of chapter 1 was that divisions of Yugoslav firms do have substantial autonomy, a major point of this chapter is that that autonomy is not unlimited. In particular, it is limited in ways that minimize the major obstacle to the efficient use of a market mechanism within the firm.

The analytical approach used in this chapter is based on Oliver Williamson's book *Markets and Hierarchies: Analysis and Antitrust Implications*, in which 'the transaction is the ultimate unit of microeconomic analysis' (1975, p. xi). This approach is particularly appropriate for the study of an economic system in which the very nature of the enterprise is undergoing a fundamental transformation.

One of the things that makes the study of the Yugoslav economy so interesting is the fact that, while some of its characteristics are those of the textbook capitalist economy, some are quite different. Applications of standard neoclassical analysis leads to some standard results (e.g. non-labor inputs are used up to the point where marginal cost equals marginal value product) and some surprising results (e.g. supply elasticity may be very low or even negative). Similarly, application of Williamson's transactional analysis to Yugoslav institutions leads to a number of interesting similarities and contrasts with capitalist economies. Virtually all of the interesting results that come out of neoclassical analysis of the Yugoslav economy are ultimately traceable to the assumption that the firm maximizes profit per worker rather than total profit. From the point of view of Williamson's approach, the interesting results are ultimately dependent on the extraordinary autonomy of the subunits of the Yugoslav enterprise.

I begin with a brief theoretical explanation of why firms exist at all, and then proceed to apply this explanation to Yugoslav firms.

Theory of the Firm

Williamson and others (see, for example, Coase, 1937; Williamson, 1970, 1971, 1975; and Dahlman, 1979) have argued that in principle *all* economic activities could be market coordinated, with every individual related to every other by market transactions. Even in the classic case of the blast furnace and rolling mill, where cost depends heavily on keeping the steel hot, one could imagine adjacent but independent enterprises concluding a contract in which one is committed to delivering to the other the hot molten steel. Indeed, we have actual examples of what might be considered extraordinarily extensive use of the market mechanism in Stigler's (1951) description of early nineteenth-century gunsmiths in Birmingham, England, and Buttrick's (1952) description of the 'inside contract system' at the Winchester Repeating Arms Co. in the United States, also late in the nineteenth century. Both involved independent firms performing a series of closely related but technologically separable tasks. Forging the barrel, making the sight, carving the wooden stock, rifling the barrel, were each done by autonomous enterprises. At the Winchester Co. the autonomous producers of various parts were even under the same roof and yet bought and sold among themselves and outsiders at market prices.

Why then are some transactions brought inside the organizational structure of the firm? Coase (1937, 1960) argues that the answer is that under certain circumstances the cost of market transactions is high, and Williamson's approach is essentially an elaboration of this explanation. The costs of market-governed transactions include (1) information costs (finding potential partners and conveying prices), (2) negotiation costs, including drawing up contracts, and (3) enforcement costs, including the inspection needed to ensure that the terms of contracts are being met. Williamson emphasizes that these costs might be relatively small were it not for the fact that in a changing world they must be borne over and over again. In his terminology, market contracts encounter two types of problems that together justify the existence of firms, that is, the by-passing of the market: bounded rationality and opportunism.

Bounded Rationality

Bounded rationality is a human characteristic. Specifically, it refers to the limit to people's ability to absorb and process information, which is the essence of decision-making. In relatively simple circumstances this limit poses no significant problem, and coordination of activities between independent economic actors can be achieved through market transactions. However, in a world of complexity and/or uncertainty, market transactions become more difficult and hence more costly in terms of the effort necessary to conclude unambiguous contracts. A complex set of activities may be difficult to describe precisely in writing. Uncertainty requires elaborate contingent claims contracts that specify the rights and obligations of all parties in each possible state of the world. In such cases, bounded rationality makes it difficult, if not impossible, to write the contracts that could in principle be made between independent economic actors. Specifying the full range of contingencies would be, if not impossible, then prohibitively costly.[2]

In the simple world of tic-tac-toe it is fairly easy to specify in advance the full decision tree, but in the complex world of chess, while theoretically conceivable, it is in practice impossible to specify the tree. Often economic activities are more like chess than they are like tic-tac-toe; hence coordination by market transactions is costly. Suppose, for example, that a firm that is buying a component from another firm asks for a minor design change that becomes appropriate because of unforeseeable external circumstances. From the point of view of social efficiency, the change should be made if the increased costs to the supplier (including any transition costs) are more than offset by the resulting increased earnings of the buyer. If this is the case, it should be possible fully to compensate the supplier for his higher costs. The problem is that the change could not have been foreseen and hence could not be specified in the contract. Therefore, the decision to make the change and the price for the modified component must be negotiated. The cost of those negotiations may swamp the potential gain and hence either the design change is not made or it is made but the gains are dissipated in the form of transactions costs.

In cases of complexity or uncertainty it may be more efficient to postpone specifying the exact obligations of each party (e.g. any possible design changes in intermediate products) until the passage of time reveals which states of the world obtain. This can be done within firms where an adaptive, sequential decision-making process ('cross your bridge as you come to it rather than crossing all possible bridges you might conceivably come to'[3]) is used without the need to reconcile divergent interests or to renegotiate contracts. The only contracts that need to be written are the much less specific agreements to merge or to establish an employer–employee relationship. Thus transactions costs are reduced below what they would be in the marketplace.

Another advantage of internal organization over market coordination in a world of complexity concerns communication. Within the firm there is likely to develop an efficient jargon or code that economizes on bounded rationality by conveying a lot of information at relatively little cost. Communication is, of course, possible *between* firms, but the need for legally binding preciseness will often raise the cost of transmitting a given amount of information.

Opportunism

The other major reason for integrating technologically separable activities into a single enterprise is to avoid problems of opportunism, which Williamson (1975, pp. 9 and 26) defines as selfishness combined with dishonesty in making and honoring contracts. In any market transaction, opportunism creates the danger that one or both parties will (1) engage in strategic manipulation of information, (2) misrepresent intentions, or (3) attempt after a contract is concluded to extract further benefits. Because of these hazards, some transactions are viewed as costly by the participants, and this explains why some firms choose vertical integration over market transactions. The social cost of opportunistic behavior (either actual or merely the perceived possibility of such behavior) may be substantial: more resources are devoted to negotiating and enforcing contracts, higher levels of inventories may be kept and there may be duplication of facilities.

Opportunism is not a significant problem as long as both sides have numerous alternative business partners to deal with. If they do, any opportunistic behavior will result in customers and/or suppliers switching to other business partners, so only firms with a very short time horizon will act that way. Only in an environment of what Williamson calls small-numbers exchange, is opportunism a serious problem. However, once contracts are made and business relationships are developed, the parties to a transaction acquire familiarity, valuable experience and specific capital, which give them important advantages over otherwise similar firms. Thus, what had been a situation of many equivalent alternatives can rapidly turn into an environment of small-numbers exchange.

Strategic manipulation of information results from what Williamson (1975, p. 31) calls information impactedness, a situation where relevant information is available to some parties to a transaction but not to others. Those who do not have the information can get it only at high cost, if at all. Under circumstances of information impactedness, the possibility of opportunistic behavior may make an economic unit reluctant to rely on the market mechanism. Suppose, for example, a firm contracts for the production of some component with another firm whose knowledge of appropriate materials and technology exceeds its own. As prices and availabilities of substitutable inputs change, decisions must be made about whether or not to adjust input proportions, which in turn may or may not affect functional characteristics of the component. But the firm producing it may manipulate the relevant information: for example, it may not call attention to a price reduction of an input or to a superior (perhaps newly available) material or process. In an environment of small-numbers exchange (i.e. very few potential suppliers) the buyer may end up with a product that is in some way non-optimal or may pay a price that exceeds what its own cost of production would be.

Misrepresentation of intentions is another possible result of the self-seeking attitude of participants in a marketplace. A firm may enter a contract knowing that it will not fully meet the expectations of its partner, possibly by not living up to implicit expectations. For example, a buyer may exaggerate the magnitude and stability of his anticipated future demand for some intermediate product. This may lead a supplier to make long-term investments that prove to be unprofitable.

Another manifestation of what Williamson calls misrepresentation of intentions is the problem of verifying the quality of intermediate products. In some cases the difficulty of doing so is the reason vertical integration is chosen rather than contracts between independent firms. This point is a variation on Alchian and Demsetz's (1972) explanation for the existence of firms. They argue that firms come into existence in order to deal with 'team production', that is, cases where the output from several inputs is greater than the sum of the outputs each input could produce alone. In such cases, A's marginal productivity is not independent of B's effort, so there are problems in simply leaving the coordination of their activities to a market mechanism and expecting each to be paid his marginal value product. The specific problem they focus on is shirking, which seems likely when productivities are not inexpensively measurable. The firm, then, comes into existence when it is impossible (or very costly) to measure the production of each of the cooperating inputs. The essential function of the firm is 'monitoring' the activities of these inputs and ensuring that each receives income commensurate with its contribution. Alchian and Demsetz's analysis is most directly applicable to labor inputs, but they also show that vertical integration might occur when it is difficult to 'meter' output for any reason, as when there is no inexpensive way to measure the productivity of the producer of an intermediate good. For example, in order to insure high quality in the production of transistors it might be more efficient (i.e. cost less) to supervise production (i.e. monitor input behavior) than to test the output. Hence a radio assembler may find it desirable to merge transistor production into his own operations.

A third aspect of opportunism is the attempt to extract benefits after a contract is concluded. The problem of post-contractual opportunistic behavior is more clearly presented by Klein, Crawford and Alchian (1978). They argue that an asset may be worth more to one *user* than to another, even if the *use* is the same. The difference between its value to the present user and its value to the second-highest-valuing user is a potentially appropriable quasi rent. Conflict over that quasi rent, or fear of such conflict, may induce the integration into a firm of activities that otherwise would be coordinated by market contract. The problem arises from the fact that, once investment has been made in an asset that is not easily moved or is very task-specific or is needed in a hurry, it may be very costly to the owner to find another buyer or very costly to the buyer to find another supplier. In such cases either party may threaten to cancel the contract unless the price is adjusted in its favor. For example, most firms are willing to rent or lease the box cars needed to ship their goods. If one owner of box cars tries to force the price above the previously agreed price, the shipper can look for another firm with which to do business. However, if the goods to be shipped are perishable, the delay may be very costly. Consequently, most meat packers, fearing such action by a supplier, own their own refrigerator cars. That is, they integrate that activity into their firms.

It could as well be the buyer who attempts to appropriate the quasi rent of a contract partner. The problem does not arise in the case of, say, computers because they are relatively easily moved and not task-specific. A renter's threat of contract cancellation is not a powerful lever in price renegotiations. Hence firms often do lease them. Obviously, refinery equipment is much more specialized and much less easily moved. We do not find manufacturers of such equipment leasing it, because once installed the user could use a threat of cancellation to force a downward adjustment of price. Rather, ownership of such assets is integrated into the firm that uses it. The same argument explains why firms lease office furniture, airplanes and railroad cars, but not elevators or bank vaults. Similarly, automobile makers contract for the supply of headlights and tires, but not body shells. For headlights and tires, manufacturers have invested in assets that can be used to produce output that can be sold to other buyers; buyers can readily purchase comparable goods from other makers. But if an independent firm were to contract to deliver Mustang fenders to Ford and made the necessary investment in dies to stamp the fenders, then both sides would face the danger of an effort to appropriate quasi rent. The independent firm's investment costs are sunk and are of little value to any buyer other than Ford. Hence it faces the danger that Ford will use a threat of contract cancellation to insist on a lower price. Conversely, because of the sales loss it would suffer while looking for another supplier and waiting for the making of new dies, Ford is vulnerable to a demand for a higher price. The same concern for timeliness explains why newspaper publishers, unlike book publishers, usually own their own printing presses. In this case, too, it is vulnerability to an effort to renegotiate price that forces newspapers but not book publishers to integrate the printing activity into the firm.

Taken together, the possibility of these various types of opportunistic behavior explains much of the actually observed integration of separable activities. Within the firm these problems of opportunism are reduced for three reasons: (1) it is difficult, if not impossible, for divisions to suppress or falsify information; (2) after integration, more effective mechanisms exist for settling disputes and for punishing selfish behavior; and (3) the parties to the transactions would not be able to claim for themselves the increased profits that would come from opportunistic behavior, and hence have little incentive to engage in such behavior.

This completes my review of why firms come into existence. It is appropriate to remember at this point that these arguments for integration have limits; they do not imply that firms should expand indefinitely, absorbing all related activities. Indeed, bounded rationality limits not only the ability to write complete contracts but also the ability to control a very large enterprise. Thus it is more efficient to leave some transactions to a market mechanism. Stigler (1951, p. 192) warns against thinking that 'transactions between firms are expensive and transactions within firms are free'. The problem always is to weigh one against the other.

Transactional Efficiency of Yugoslav Divisionalization

The essence of Williamson's argument is that it is efficient to bring some transactions inside the enterprise because bounded rationality and opportunism make market transactions costly. The major question to which we now turn is whether the extensive subunit autonomy characteristic of Yugoslav enterprises interferes with that efficiency. That is, how costly is the Yugoslav decision to negotiate transactions that capitalist firms have, apparently for good reason, assigned to administrative decision-making?

At the outset it should be clear that transactions between subdivisions of a Yugoslav firm do not exactly fit either of Williamson's two categories. They are neither the pure market transactions that involve exchange between totally autonomous entities, nor the hierarchical exchange in which 'a single administrative entity spans both sides of the transaction, some form of subordination prevails, and, typically, consolidated ownership obtains' (Williamson, 1975, p. xi). Rather they are a hybrid with some characteristics of each: the transaction is between largely autonomous divisions that are nonetheless part of a single entity that spans both sides of the transaction. Interdivisional negotiations result in two types of contracts: the more general 'self-management agreement' sets out the basic operating rules governing income distribution, planning procedures and marketing and investment strategies; the more detailed annual plans specify the prices and quantities of goods and services to be traded within the enterprise. As described in chapter 1, some enterprises are more tightly knit and central management is able to implement unified strategies and procedures. In others, the sense of solidarity and reciprocity is weaker and the center exercises less control. But the law requires that in all enterprises final authority rests with the divisions, which must approve all contracts, both the general and the specific. Thus, in every case the process is essentially one of negotiation among separate units. Only in so far as each is legally bound by decisions jointly made is there subordination to the center.[4] The concept of consolidated ownership does not apply because of the Yugoslav notion of social ownership; furthermore, technically it is the divisions not the enterprise that manage all assets. There may, however, be a consciousness of joint control over property.

In these circumstances how appropriate is Williamson's claim that bringing technologically separable activities into the enterprise economizes on bounded rationality? If two distinct activities are brought into a Yugoslav firm, does that reduce the cost of transactions between them? The answer to this question is not a simple yes or no. Since Yugoslav law requires that distinguishable activities be constituted as separate divisions, and since no higher authority can impose prices, quantities, conditions, etc. on transactions between them, they will still have to bear some of the costs of market transactions. Most important, the costs of periodically negotiating a price remain. This is true even in those cases, discussed in chapter 1, where a major function of transfer prices is income redistribution. Further, their freedom to buy and sell outside the firm means divisions will incur the expense of finding potential partners and conveying prices. Even if the divisions were to restrict themselves to dealing within the firm, and thus were spared the costs of frequently searching the marketplace for partners, at contract renewal time the divisions are likely to do a certain amount of market searching, if only to get a benchmark for the internal price. Thus, the cost of transactions between divisions does not at first appear to be lower than that of transactions between independent firms.

However, it can be argued that in some respects long-term contracts are equivalent to merger. For example, Kessler and Stern (1959, p. 2) argue that 'contract integration' is an alternative to 'ownership integration' as a means of achieving vertical coordination. 'Contractual arrangements aimed at coordinating the supply of materials or disposal of output frequently affect the contracting firms, as well as the rest of the industry, in much the same way as ownership of suppliers or outlets does.' Indeed, in many cases American antitrust law treats certain types of contracts (e.g. requirement, whole output, exclusive dealing, franchise, consignment, and agency agreements) as forms of vertical integration. On the other hand, Alchian and Demsetz (1972, p. 783) argue that 'long-term contracts . . . are not an essential attribute of the firm'. The firm, they say (p. 794), 'is simply a contractual structure subject to continuous renegotiation'. These two positions are not really in conflict. Taken together, what they mean is that it is possible to have long-term contracts without creating a firm, and it is possible to create a firm without having long-term contracts. In any case, long-term contracts may reduce the cost of using a market. Perhaps in this way divisions of Yugoslav firms get some of the benefits of merger while retaining their autonomy.

Kessler and Stern (1959, p. 4n) illustrate a typical American business viewpoint by quoting from a text for purchasing agents (they are quoting Heinritz, 1947, p. 314):

> Successful subcontracting . . . regards the operations of the supplier as part of a continuous process, leading up to and including the operations in the buyer's own plant. . . . So far as the subcontracts are concerned, the supplier's operations are a part of his customer's operation, even though they are carried on under a different roof and a different management.

Representative of this attitude is General Electric, which is known to be especially thorough in coordinating the activities of its subcontractors. It sometimes helps them tool up and often provides them with technical assistance. In many cases GE finds that a long-term contract achieves all of the benefits of outright ownership.

In Yugoslav firms, interdivisional contracts that specify prices and quantities are usually not longer-term than interfirm contracts. That is, on this basis alone the fact of bringing two activities into the firm, in and of itself, does not improve transactional efficiency. However, on matters other than price and quantity it seems that intrafirm contracts do tend to be longer and the relationship closer. Thus they fit quite nicely what MacMillan and Farmer (1979, p. 277) describe as 'collaborative dealing' between separate buyers and sellers, by which they mean such things as extensive exchange of information, willingness to accommodate changes and coordinated use of inventories and warehouses. Talking about capitalist industrial markets, MacMillan and Farmer claim that the organizational viability studied by Cyert and March is enhanced by such 'closer vertical relationships between buyers and sellers'. These are particularly valuable in fields like electronics, where collaboration can reduce the effects of the uncertainty that usually accompanies rapid technological change.

This closeness in the relationship between contracting partners strengthens the effectiveness of contract integration in Yugoslav firms. The specific knowledge that comes from long experience reduces negotiation costs and facilitates efficient communication. The practice of setting intermediate prices as percentages of a final price obviates the need for frequent renegotiations in times of inflation. With experience, other rules of thumb evolve that reduce the time necessary to agree on price. Also, in so far as divisions expect to maintain long-term business relations, their costs of searching for partners may be reduced. Further, it could be argued that the longer the period covered by a contract the lower are the average transactions costs of coordinating these activities (that is, the transactions costs are spread over a greater volume of goods or services). On the other hand, there is also the possibility that longer-term contracts will have to deal with more uncertainty and hence may be more difficult (costly) to negotiate.

Obviously, it is not possible to build a strong argument for the efficiency of Yugoslav enterprise structure entirely in terms of long-term contracts. To some extent Yugoslav enterprises use them, and hence there is no conflict with that purpose for creating firms. However, the long-term stable relationship between activities is not in principle the primary *raison d'être* for firms. A stronger case for efficiency can be built in terms of the Alchian and Demsetz analysis, which focuses on metering input and output; in this respect it is quite clear that the structure of Yugoslav enterprises does not defeat the purpose of creating firms. Alchian and Demsetz claim that it is more efficient to coordinate within the firm activities that do not have a measurable output and to allow the market to coordinate activities that do. This is precisely what Yugoslav law prescribes, except that it is *divisions* not enterprises that monitor the activities of inputs whose output is not easily measurable. As explained in chapter 1, the law explicitly states that divisions are *defined* as Alchian and Demsetz would recommend, namely, as economic activities whose output is measurable. Thus, giving them autonomy does not cause problems in terms of measuring their productivity. Activities that involve team production are kept within a division where contributions are metered and income is distributed in some non-market fashion.

Solidarity and Adaptive, Sequential Decision-making
In seeking an answer to the question of whether the structure of Yugoslav enterprises interferes with the very purpose of creating firms, there is another consideration that may be more important than any mentioned so far. That is the 'goodwill' that encourages businessmen to run the risk of contractual incompleteness rather than bear the higher transactions costs of complete specification. While this may be relevant to inter-enterprise relations as well, it is especially important within the Yugoslav firm. What the Yugoslavs call the 'solidarity' of the enterprise may substantially lower transaction costs between divisions.

This brings us to a fundamental difference between a long-term contract and merger: the former usually does not allow the adaptive, sequential decision-making that economizes on bounded rationality. If Yugoslav divisions not only retained their autonomy, but also had to agree *in advance* on everything that each is obligated to do, they would not benefit from the reduced transaction costs of administrative decision-making. But could we not argue that, within the enterprise 'family', contracts do not necessarily have to specify the full range of contingencies? That is, within the firm can problems of divergent interests somehow be reconciled even in the absence of complete specification? As long as no higher authority can impose a settlement on a dispute, unforeseen circumstances would seem to require costly haggling and possibly socially inefficient behavior. But is it not possible somehow to write the original contract so as to avoid reopening the negotiations? Certainly any specific changes that may be foreseen can be settled in advance and written into the contract. But the problem of bounded rationality is just that many changes cannot be foreseen. Can there not be some general scheme for adapting to changes without encountering further transactions costs? Williamson suggests a solution and then says that it will not work. Perhaps in the Yugoslav environment it will. Indeed, I argue that the Yugoslav enterprise's self-management agreement is exactly the solution Williamson seeks: it enables autonomous units to engage in adaptive, sequential decision-making.

Williamson's proposed solution is a contract that specifies that if any proposed change will raise joint profit then the change will be made and the increase in joint profit will be divided between the parties in proportions specified in the contract. There is evidence that this will lead to joint profit maximization and a Pareto optimal allocation of resources.[5] In the Yugoslav case, this means both divisions will have an incentive to go along with any change that is in the interests of the firm. Indeed, Williamson (1975, pp. 92–3) admits that, with complete and accurate information about the effects on both parties, 'the incomplete contract does not appear to impede efficiency or occasion costly haggling. Rather the contrivance of a general clause and sharing rule seems to give the parties to an incomplete long-term contract the requisite incentives to adapt efficiently in a joint-profit maximizing way'. The problem (which Williamson sees as fatal) arises in accurately determining the effect of the change on the profit of each division. The buyer is likely to understate the benefit to him and the supplier will exaggerate the cost to him. That is, opportunism interferes.

It seems, then, that it is opportunism, not bounded rationality, that presents the greater obstacle to transactional efficiency in contracts between independent units. This is extremely important. If the problem of opportunistic distortion of expected costs and profit were overcome in the Yugoslav firm, then with proper use of sharing clauses it would be possible to use long-term contracts to organize efficient transactions between divisions. We know that there is a strong sense of solidarity among the divisions of the Yugoslav firm. To the extent that that sense of 'being part of one family' reduces opportunistic behavior, the autonomous divisions of a Yugoslav enterprise can rely on long-term contracts without loss of efficiency. The nature of that solidarity was discussed in chapter 1 and will turn up again in chapter 6. I turn now to a more formal look at the implications of reduced opportunism in the Yugoslav environment.

Opportunism in the Yugoslav Firm
In terms of opportunism, Williamson cites three advantages for intrafirm transactions over market transactions. The Yugoslav firm can claim all three, although with some qualifications to the third. The first concerns the feasibility of opportunistic behavior. When both parties to a transaction are in the same firm it is more difficult to suppress or falsify information. This argument is certainly appropriate in the Yugoslav case, where disclosure regulations are quite extensive. Workers in each division know quite precisely the income level of workers in other divisions, and information regarding the expected impact of anticipated actions must be shared. These rules can reasonably be expected to limit opportunistic behavior.

The second of Williamson's advantages for intrafirm transactions is that integration provides effective mechanisms for settling disputes and punishing opportunistic behavior. While the Yugoslav firm does not have a head office that can impose settlements and fire division directors, this may not be very important. Alchian and Demsetz (1972, p. 777) assert that the common belief in the strong central authority of a capitalist firm 'is delusion'.

> The firm . . . has no power of fiat, no authority, no disciplinary action any different in the slightest degree from ordinary market contracting between any two people. I can 'punish' you only by withholding future business or by seeking redress in courts. . . . That is exactly all that my employer can do. He can fire or sue, just as I can fire my grocer by stopping purchases from him or sue him.

Alchian and Demsetz are referring primarily to the relationship between firm and employees rather than to the relationship between divisions of the firm. But the point remains valid that the primary 'threat' that disciplines the various participants in a firm is the prospect that others will withhold future business. Because divisions are free to buy and sell outside, the same 'threat' is present in the Yugoslav firm. Furthermore, although enterprise headquarters cannot impose settlements, it can facilitate agreements and exercise effective pressure. The central workers' council provides a forum where disagreements are aired and where behavior considered selfish or dishonest can be exposed. Certainly, the Yugoslav enterprise is not entirely or even essentially identical to the neoclassical firm Alchian and Demsetz describe. In particular, the central workers' council does not make bilateral contracts with all other parties, so it is not in a position to punish divisions. But it does help settle disagreements and does reduce opportunism below what it would be if the parties to a transaction were not in the same firm. While it cannot be said that opportunism in the Yugoslav firm is as low as opportunism in the capitalist firm, the important point here is that transactions *within* the Yugoslav firm encounter less opportunism than transactions *between* Yugoslav firms.

There are also a number of factors that Klein *et al.* (1978) mention as preventing the post-contractual opportunism on which they focus. Several of them fit the Yugoslav firm exactly. For example, they mention that social sanctions are effective in business relations among members of the same church or country club. Certainly this applies to the Yugoslav firm, where actions recognized as opportunistic will be subject to substantial opposition from other divisions, the Party and the community. They also suggest that a compulsory arbitration clause in the contract can be important. A regular arbitration procedure is a permanent part of the organizational structure of most Yugoslav firms. Furthermore, the law specifically prohibits any division from cancelling on short notice a contract with a sister division if there is demonstrable harm to the firm. This does not eliminate, but at least reduces the likelihood of the post-contractual opportunistic behavior discussed by Klein et al.

Williamson's third argument is the most difficult to apply in the Yugoslav context. It is that integration reduces the incentive to engage in opportunistic behavior because each party is not able to claim for itself any increased profit. In the short run, this does not apply to a Yugoslav division, which may well succeed in keeping for itself additional profit that results from its own opportunistic behavior. However, the system of income distribution peculiar to the Yugoslav enterprise is such that in the long run each worker's income depends on both the profit of his own division and the profit of the entire enterprise. The mechanism varies from one firm to another and a number of examples are discussed in detail in chapter 6; but at this point we need only note that if one division consistently earns income substantially higher than those in other divisions of the same firm, then there will be strong, and probably effective, pressure to adjust transfer prices in a way that will result in a more nearly uniform income distribution across divisions. The fact that, in the long run, a division cannot keep for itself profits that exceed the profits of sister divisions reduces the incentive to engage in opportunistic behavior when dealing with those divisions.

Obviously, an extremely important empirical question is whether this hybrid system of income distribution can achieve both of its goals, namely, providing incentives for individuals to work hard in the short run (Tyson, 1979) and suppressing opportunistic behavior through long-run adjustments. To the extent that it succeeds in the latter, the feasibility of writing efficient long-term contracts is increased.

Finally, we might point out that in the Yugoslav environment there is an additional limit on opportunistic behavior: the freedom of divisions to buy and sell outside the enterprise reduces the problem of small-numbers exchange. As pointed out earlier, to some extent long-term contracts tend to undermine this by giving established suppliers an advantage, but this freedom should not be entirely discounted. Thus, in Yugoslavia, even within the enterprise, opportunistic behavior may provoke sister divisions into finding other partners.

Opportunism and Conflict in Yugoslav Economics

It is ironic that Yugoslavia has developed a corporate structure that reduces opportunistic behavior when in fact there seems to be a widespread belief in the basic harmony of interests within the economy. Possibly, one might argue that this belief *results* from the effective operation of this corporate structure. But, to the contrary, the common belief seems to be that there is no need to be concerned about opportunism. Both the writing of economists and the actual legislation that determines the structure of enterprises emphasize the common interest of all subunits in reducing costs and increasing sales. This has obscured the underlying conflict that is the focus of much of Williamson's analysis. The Yugoslavs have failed to see, as John R. Commons (1934, pp. 6–7) did, that 'cooperation does not arise from a presupposed harmony of interests...' but rather 'from the necessity of creating... order... out of the conflict of interests among the hoped-for cooperators.... Hence, harmony is not a presupposition of economics – it is a consequence of collective action designed to maintain rules that shall govern the conflicts.'

The legislation that divisionalized Yugoslav firms (especially the Constitution of 1974 and the Law on Associated Labor of 1976) is not very specific regarding the regulation of conflict. With respect to internal transfer prices and other ways of dividing up enterprise profits, it says little more than that the parties shall jointly agree on something fair (see, for example, Law on Associated Labor, article 86). One might argue that this reflects a conscious decision to leave such operational details to the enterprises themselves, but then we would hope to find in the economics journals and textbooks considerable attention focused on the search for concrete procedures for dealing with the conflict. Unfortunately, in these sources we usually find the same willingness to rely on common interests, good intentions and the participants' ability to agree on what is fair. In discussions of the distribution of income among divisions there is usually a casual confidence that self-management agreements will settle the matter equitably (see, for example, Vacić, 1978, p. 14).

What is not adequately recognized in abstract discussion is that if one division gets a bigger slice of the pie there is less left for the others. Of course, it is not always a zero sum game; the size of the pie need not be fixed. But the need to find efficient ways to divide up the pie has not received explicit attention. The same problem arises in connection with planning, which has received increasing attention in recent years. Here, too, there seems to be a belief that if only the parties to market transactions are brought together to make decisions in advance, then price fluctuations and supply problems will disappear and an equitable distribution of income will be achieved. Fortunately, in actual business practice firms do establish viable decision-making mechanisms.

Summary

Because of their extensive divisionalization, Yugoslav firms bear many of the costs of using a market. In terms of information and negotiation costs, the system of autonomous subunits does appear costly. However, Williamson tells us that the major efficiency advantage of bringing transactions into the firm rather than leaving them to the market lies in the fact that this solves the problem of contractual incompleteness: that is, bounded rationality makes it impossible to specify contracts completely and opportunism makes incomplete contracts hazardous and possibly socially inefficient. In Yugoslavia, the enterprise does not eliminate the contracts, but rather it constitutes a shell within which a market can operate with incomplete contracts. Indeed, we can define the Yugoslav enterprise as a shell within which opportunism is reduced. By reducing opportunistic behavior, the enterprise allows autonomous work units to relate to one another through long-term contracts despite the contractual incompleteness that is inevitable, given bounded rationality. With opportunism considerably reduced, sharing clauses can be used to allow adaptive, sequential decision-making as uncertainties disappear with the passage of time. Thus, more complicated and longer-term coordination can take place. This means that the scope of the enterprise (i.e. the number and variety of transactions it encompasses) is very important. This is especially true with regard to a particular type of contract, namely, capital flows, which is the subject of the next chapter. At this point, the important conclusion is that bringing technologically separable activities together in a single firm does reduce some of the costs of transactions between them.

Notes

1 See, for example, Stigler (1958) and Williamson (1975), p. 252. To be precise, Stigler applied his survivor principle to firm size rather than corporate structure.
2 Meade (1971, p. 183) discusses the impossibility of a complete set of conditional forward markets. See also Arrow (1969, p. 51). Both are cited in Williamson (1975), p. 24.
3 Chernoff and Moses (1959), p. 192, cited in Williamson (1975), p. 25.
4 The Yugoslav firm does encompass some hierarchical relationships that do involve subordination and administrative control. But these are *within* divisions, while my analysis is concerned with the relationship *between* divisions.
5 Hurwicz (1973), pp. 25–6. See also the literature on bilateral monopoly in which an accepted result is that the joint-profit maximizing quantity will be produced but price will be indeterminant.

5 Investment Decisions in the Divisionalized Firm

Introduction

The purpose of this chapter is to investigate some theoretical issues relevant to corporate investment decisions. Of course, it is entirely possible, even likely, that these issues will be outweighed by more practical considerations: if workers believe that new equipment is necessary to preserve their jobs in the face of competition, they will vote to invest despite any theoretical arguments to the contrary. But that does not mean we are not interested in what theoretical biases there may be. In the next chapter, I take a more empirical approach and look at some case studies.

Much of the theoretical literature on investment in labor-managed economies concerns a bias that may make workers reluctant to invest their own money in their firm. This in turn is often taken to mean that the amount of investment undertaken by the labor-managed firm is heavily dependent on whether projects are funded with retained profits (i.e. the money that workers are reluctant to invest) or with outside credit, which presumably they are more willing to spend. If the source of funding is important, then it would seem that divisionalization, with the possibility of one division funding another division's project, would substantially alter the firm's investment behavior. That is, each division might treat a loan from a sister division as outside credit and therefore invest more than it would with its own funds. However, careful analysis of the institutional characteristics of the Yugoslav system shows that investment decisions there are not likely to be as sensitive to type of financing as the literature suggests. Therefore, the significance of interdivisional capital flows is less than might reasonably be expected. Further, under careful examination the willingness of divisions to lend to one another also turns out to be less than one might expect. Nonetheless, there are circumstances under which interdivisional lending will take place.

In dealing with this topic I discuss some of the factors that are relevant to the division's decision to borrow or lend. In many circumstances these factors influence interdivisional capital flows even when they are also inter-enterprise flows. That is, whether or not the borrowing and lending divisions happen to be in the same enterprise often is not important in this respect.

The chapter has three parts. The first presents the well-known Furubotn/Pejovich bias in the investment decisions of labor-managed firms and suggests an alternative interpretation that, though mathematically equivalent, has some logical and intuitive advantages over the original version. I also bring inflation into the analysis. After arguing that inflation is not a consequence of the Furubotn/Pejovich bias, I argue that it is likely to be the source of an opposite bias. The second part deals with the effect of the availability of borrowed funds on the type of financing and the amount of investment undertaken by the firm. It also suggests an institutional change that might lessen the impact of the Furubotn/Pejovich bias. The third part focuses on interdivisional lending. After presenting the argument that loans between divisions may increase investment, it shows that institutional arrangements work in the opposite direction. Attention is drawn to the importance of the length of time of loans, something that is not given much attention in the literature.

At the start of any discussion of investment decisions in Yugoslavia it is important to point out a basic institutional characteristic of the Yugoslav system: the firm is required by law to maintain the value of its capital. That is, it must pay into its own business fund each year an amount of money equal to that year's depreciation on its current capital stock. Money in the business fund may be used for investment but may not be distributed for individual consumption. This principle is based on the belief that the capital in every firm belongs to society as a whole and may not be consumed by those who work with it. One way of looking at this is to say that the Yugoslav firm is continually converting physical assets into financial assets: as machinery wears out the firm sets aside from current revenue an amount of money equal to that depreciation. These financial assets are periodically reconverted into physical assets (e.g. the firm buys a machine), but they may not be distributed as personal income.

Another way to look at this is to say that once the decision is made to undertake a project, the Yugoslav firm is committed perpetually to continue that project, or some other project of equivalent financial magnitude. By contrast, a capitalist firm has in addition the options of (1) allowing an asset to wear out without replacing it, thus gradually ending the project, and (2) selling the asset, without making an equivalent purchase, thus at one stroke ending the project. That is, for the capitalist firm investment involves a continuous decision-making process; on any day it can be partially or entirely undone, and the total stock of capital is variable downward as well as upward. For the Yugoslav firm, a decision to invest entails a commitment to reinvest and the amount of capital is variable only upward.

It is important to make clear that this capital maintenance requirement, which underlies all of the results of this chapter, is not a characteristic of all labor-managed economic systems. For example, in the plywood firms in the northwestern part of the United States and the complex network of enterprises at Mondragon in Spain, co-op members accumulate cash value that they can claim when they retire or quit. Thus the firm's capital can decrease as well as increase, although it is likely to do so more gradually than in a capitalist firm because it is tied to the withdrawal of members.

The Furubotn/Pejovich Bias

The well-known bias in labor-managed investment decisions has been described by Furubotn and Pejovich in numerous articles (Furubotn and Pejovich, 1970, 1973; Furubotn, 1971, 1974, 1976, 1980a, 1980b; Pejovich, 1973). The essence of their argument is that workers do not have full ownership rights over the assets of the firm and hence cannot recover the principal amount of their investment in the firm's assets at the end of their time horizon. In individual savings accounts, on the other hand, workers can reclaim the principal as well as interest. Consequently, they will invest in the firm only if the prospective rate of return is higher, by at least a certain amount, than the rate of interest paid on savings accounts.

Furubotn and Pejovich's formal statement varies slightly from one article to another, but the point they are making is the same. It can be stated in either of two ways, both of which express the relationship between s, the rate of interest that can be earned on individual (owned) assets, and r, the equivalent rate of return on collective (non-owned) assets. 'Equivalent' means a rate that makes workers indifferent between investing in owned and non-owned assets.

First, the rate of return on non-owned assets can be said to be equivalent to the rate earned on owned assets if the present value of the stream of income from each dollar invested in the firm equals the present value of the stream of income from each dollar put in a savings account. For a time horizon T, the present value of the savings account is

$$\frac{s}{1+s} + \frac{s}{(1+s)^2} + \ldots + \frac{s+1}{(1+s)^T} = 1.$$

The present value of the dollar invested in the firm is

$$\frac{r}{1+s} + \frac{r}{(1+s)^2} + \ldots + \frac{r}{(1+s)^T} = \sum_{t=1}^{T} \frac{r}{(1+s)^t}.$$

Therefore, if and only if

$$\sum_{t=1}^{T} \frac{r}{(1+s)^t} = 1, \tag{1}$$

then r and s are equivalent. The reason r and s are different is evident from the last term in the two series: the '1' in one case but not the other reflects the return of the original dollar invested.

A second way of expressing the relation between s and r is to look at funds available for consumption at some future time T. If a worker puts a dollar in a savings account and leaves it and the interest there, it will accumulate to $(1+s)^T$. On the other hand, if he invests a dollar in the firm, it will accumulate to $(1+r)^T - 1$ (because the principal is not recoverable). If

$$(1+s)^T = (1+r)^T - 1, \tag{2}$$

then r and s are equivalent; that is, the worker is indifferent between investing in owned and non-owned assets. For a given s, the rate of return in the firm must be at least this r in order to induce workers to invest in their firm.

The difference between (1) and (2) is that the former is based on the present value of a prospective stream of income and the latter is based on the future value of a dollar invested now. Economists by training tend to think in terms of present value, while one might argue that workers are more likely to ask how much they will get to spend later for each dollar invested now. But that should not matter since either method can be used to calculate the r that is equivalent to a given s. Indeed, the two have generally been regarded as alternative statements of the same principle. However, there is an important difference, which has eluded many readers.

The first expression discounts future income back to the present at rate s, for both types of investment, while the second compounds earnings into the future at rate r for non-owned assets only. Consequently, when we try to plug Furubotn and Pejovich's numerical examples into the second formulation we find that they do not fit. Table 5.1 shows the values of r that are equivalent to a 5 per cent rate of interest on savings accounts. Columns 1 and 2 show r calculated using methods (1) and (2), respectively. The reason that method (2) yields lower r's is that it assumes that earnings on non-owned assets are compounded into the future at r, which is higher than s. That is, if the return on investment in the firm is compounded at r instead of at s, then the gap between r and s will be smaller.

Table 5.1 *Investment in Non-owned Assets: Rates of Return Equivalent to a 5 per cent Rate of Interest on Savings*

T	(1) Present value of stream of income	(2) Funds available for consumption at time T	(3)
	$1 = \sum_{t=1}^{T} \dfrac{r}{(1+s)^t}$	$(1+s)^T = (1+r)^T - 1$	$(1+s)^T = r \dfrac{(1+s)^T - 1}{s}$
1	1.05	1.05	1.05
5	0.23	0.18	0.23
6	0.19	0.15	0.19
10	0.13	0.10	0.13
20	0.08	0.07	0.08

Since r is what Furubotn and Pejovich refer to as the critical rate of return, i.e. the minimum return that will induce workers to invest in their firm, the fact that it may be lower than implied by expression (1) is significant. If (2) more accurately represents the decision criterion than expression (1), then there will be more investment in the firm than Furubotn and Pejovich suggest. There remains a bias in favor of owned assets, but it is weaker. An important question then is whether compounding at r is likely to be an option available in the Yugoslav economy.

It is hard to imagine in concrete terms how the earnings on a project could be compounded at rate r. Since r usually represents the return on some tangible project (as opposed to a financial instrument), reinvesting the earnings at the same rate is possible only if the marginal rate of return in physical assets is constant. But it is not always feasible to reproduce the same project on a smaller scale: even buying more of the same machines but in smaller quantities or scaled down versions or perhaps building an additional wing onto a new factory is not likely to yield the same rate of return.

But an even greater problem with compounding at rate r is the fact that, if the earnings on non-owned assets were reinvested (compounded), the workers would then lose the right to consume those earnings and would be left with nothing but the interest earned in some final period.

A more plausible assumption is that the earnings on non-owned assets are distributed to the workers each period[1] and are deposited in their savings accounts where they are compounded over time at rate s. When invested at rate s, one dollar per period accumulates to $\frac{[(1+s)^T - 1]}{s}$, so r dollars per period (the return on each dollar invested in non-owned assets) will accumulate to $r \frac{[(1+s)^T - 1]}{s}$. Therefore, for owned and non-owned assets to provide an equal amount of funds available for consumption at time T, the following must hold:

$$(1+s)^T = r \cdot \frac{(1+s)^T - 1}{s}.$$

The left side of this equation represents the funds available for consumption at time T if one dollar is invested in a savings account and left to accumulate at rate of interest s. The right side represents funds available at time T if one dollar is invested in non-owned assets and the return of r per period accumulates at rate s. This can be rewritten as

$$r = s \frac{(1+s)^T}{(1+s)^T - 1} \qquad (3)$$

This is mathematically different from expression (2) and provides a neater statement of the relationship between s and r than either (1) or (2). It also makes quite clear two of Furubotn and Pejovich's conclusions, namely, that if $T = 1$ then $r = s + 1$ and that as T becomes larger r approaches s. Column 3 of Table 5.1 shows that this formulation, although based on a different interpretation, is mathematically equivalent to expression (1).

Evidently, if the discounting in the present value calculation and the compounding in the future value calculation are done using the same interest rate, than they yield the same value of r. However, there is room for argument over the appropriate rate to use. In most of their articles Furubotn and Pejovich discount using the rate paid on savings accounts, but in some variants they instead use an adjusted r, which may or may not be equal to s (Furubotn and Pejovich, 1970, p. 451; Furubotn, 1976, p. 116).

It is clear from expression (3) that, if the workers' time horizon T is less than infinite, r will be greater than s; that is, the equivalent rate of return on non-owned assets will be greater than the rate of interest paid on savings accounts. Clearly, the size of the gap between r and s

depends on s and T. For any given T, the larger is s the smaller is the relative gap (because the larger is s the larger are both the numerator and denominator of the fraction and the smaller, in relative terms, is the difference between them). Similarly, for any given s, the larger is T the smaller is the gap (again because both numerator and denominator get larger while the difference between them remains exactly 1).

Inflation

Before turning to the second part, we ought to consider another matter that is relevant to the relationship between r and s. A major thrust of many of Furubotn's articles is that, because of the bias against reinvestment in the firm, workers will borrow rather than self-finance expansion of the firm and that this in turn will cause inflation. In fact, the bias itself does not necessarily lead to inflation. It is true that inflation can result from an excess of total investment over total savings. But what Furubotn and Pejovich have shown is that workers will in some cases choose savings accounts over corporate investment, not consumption over savings. That is, they have shown a reluctance of workers to engage in a *particular kind* of saving. Bank-financed investment need not be any more inflationary than self-financed investment as long as the total amount of worker savings is adequate. Stephen (1980, p. 798) shows that any retardation of saving in the economy occurs only 'if the interest paid by the banks to their depositors is insufficient to bring forth the level of saving necessary to meet the demand from potential borrowers'. Similarly, Tyson (1980, pp. 78–84) argues that Yugoslav inflation is the result of unrealistic wages and excessive money creation by the banks. What actually seems to be the cause of inflation in Furubotn's discussion is government action to stimulate expansion. Indeed, when he is explicit on this point, the strongest statement he can make is that 'it seems likely that the government will ... [put] excessive credit into the system, thus generating inflation' (1980b, p. 803n). He admits (p. 802) that when interest rates are adjusted correctly 'the amount workers save is precisely equal to the amount the firm invests' and that the total amount invested can 'mimic' the capitalist solution.

Regardless of whether inflation is a consequence of the Furubotn/Pejovich bias, it brings us to an issue that has not been mentioned in the literature on Yugoslav investment decisions. Furubotn and Pejovich admit (1970, p. 447) that alternative forms of investment may differ in terms of 'risk level, liquidity, etc.' but they do not explicitly recognize that inflation is likely to cause a systematic bias in *favor* of investment in real, and hence non-owned, assets.[2] Clearly, if they claim that inflation is a consequence of their analysis, they should consider its impact on that analysis. In a discussion that focuses on the effects of time horizons in investment decisions, changes in the price level should not be ignored.

In a labor-managed economy, virtually all individually owned financial assets are savings accounts, in which principal and interest are measured in nominal terms, i.e. are not adjusted for inflation. In real terms, the return on investment is equal to the nominal interest rate minus the rate of inflation. Non-owned investments, on the other hand, are in the form of real assets (factories, production machinery, etc.), which pay a return in the form of goods and services produced. In general, we can expect the prices of what is produced by the investment to rise with the overall price level. Thus the return is essentially indexed for inflation and the real rate of return equals the nominal rate.

This differential effect of inflation on owned and non-owned assets works in the opposite direction from the bias shown by Furubotn and Pejovich. To take as an example some quite plausible numbers, suppose that savings accounts earn a nominal rate of interest of 8 per cent. The Furubotn/Pejovich criterion suggests that workers with a five-year time horizon would need to expect at least a 25 per cent return $(= 0.08 \, [1.08^5 / (1.08^5 - 1)])$ in order to invest in the firm. However, suppose that the rate of inflation is 15 per cent and the return on industrial assets is 12 per cent. Then the real return on owned assets is $- 7$ per cent $(= 8 - 15)$. A dollar invested in a savings account will in five years have dwindled in real purchasing power to less than 70 cents $(0.93^5 = 0.696)$, while in the same five years a dollar invested in non-owned industrial assets will also make available approximately[3] 70 cents for consumption $(0.12 \, [\, (1.08^5 - 1)/0.08] = 0.7040)$. Thus for workers with a time horizon of more than five years a return of 12 per cent, not 25 per cent, is sufficient to induce them to choose non-owned assets.

The point is quite simple: in times of inflation, workers in any type of economic system prefer to invest in real assets. In socialist economies, virtually the only way to do so is through enterprise reinvestment.

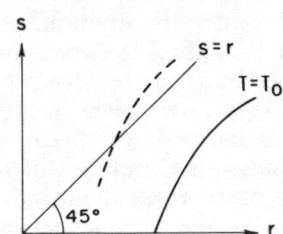

Figure 5.1

Investment Decisions in the Divisionalized Firm 83

The effect of inflation on Furubotn and Pejovich's diagrams is easily shown. Their (1970) curve that plots s against r for a given time horizon (Figure 5.1, which reproduces the first quadrant of their figure 6) will shift leftward and may in fact go above the $s = r$ 45° line. That is, inflation may induce workers to invest in non-owned assets rather than owned assets even if the nominal rate of interest on the latter is higher than the return on the former. If that curve does intersect the $s = r$ line, then for that time horizon there is exactly one rate of interest on savings accounts that equals the equivalent return on corporate investment. At this particular value, and for this particular time horizon, the Furubotn/Pejovich bias against non-owned assets is exactly offset by the inflation bias in favor of non-owned assets.

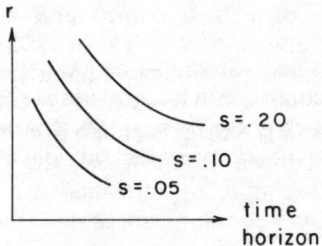

Figure 5.2

Figure 5.2 (which reproduces their figure 5) shows the downward sloping curves that relate r to the time horizon (each corresponding to a given value of s). The effect of inflation is to shift downward the entire family of curves because, in order to induce workers to invest in the firm, a smaller rate of return on corporate investment is necessary with inflation than without inflation. The fact that the slope of the curve in Figure 5.1 is greater than 1 reflects the fact that a change in s will cause a somewhat smaller change in the equivalent r. Therefore, the downward shift of the family of curves in Figure 5.2 will be somewhat less than the rate of inflation.

The Importance of Borrowed Funds

Unless inflation fully offsets the Furubotn/Pejovich bias, there will remain some bias against investment in the firm. Let us go on to consider an implication of this bias. Workers will undertake projects within the enterprise only if the rate of return on those projects is greater than or equal to the critical rate r, which is higher than the savings account rate s. That is, projects that earn rates of return greater than s but less than r – projects that would be undertaken in a capitalist system because they earn more than the market interest rate – will not be financed by workers in the labor-managed environment. Thus, if retained earnings within the enterprise were the only source of funding, the total amount of investment would be less than in a comparable capitalist firm.

However, if funds can be borrowed, the amount of investment undertaken by the self-managed firm might not be less than the amount undertaken by the capitalist firm. Because of the possibility of interdivisional financing, analysis of response to the availability of credit is crucial to the study of the multidivisional firm. We want to know whether the availability of interdivisional loans would increase divisions' investment levels.

The possibility of the firm borrowing to finance investment in fixed assets is at the core of a lively controversy between Furubotn and Stephen. (See Furubotn 1974, 1976, 1980b; Stephen, 1980). Furubotn argues that the possibility of bank funding will eliminate or sharply reduce workers' willingness to divert money from consumption to reinvestment in the firm. Stephen argues that this need not be the case, that under certain circumstances the availability of loans will cause little or no reduction in self-financed investment by the firm. Furubotn replies that the circumstances under which firms will choose self-financing over bank borrowing are very unlikely to occur. Both seem to argue that the availability of credit is likely to increase total investment.

At the center of the Furubotn–Stephen controversy is a diagram in which the horizontal axis measures amounts of saving and investment and the vertical axis measures rates of interest. Furubotn and Stephen agree that the supply curve of corporate savings (i.e. funds that could have been distributed as wages) for investment in physical assets is a kinked line like r^*BS' in Figure 5.3. For any point on that line, the abscissa measures the amount of corporate savings that workers are willing to reinvest in real assets when the marginal return on those assets is given by the ordinate of that point. It is assumed that the time horizon T is fixed and that r^* is equivalent to the (fixed) s paid on savings accounts. The horizontal segment results from the assumption that at rates of return below r^* workers will not invest at all in the firm, while at rates above r^* they will switch into the firm the entire amount that they otherwise would have put into savings accounts. The sloping segment of the line is above the conventional savings function by an amount equal to the gap between r and s.

In order to get to the heart of the disagreement, let us assume that the firm will undertake an amount of investment in physical assets equal to at least distance OF. The question is whether a labor-managed firm will choose to borrow at rate of interest i. The alternative is to pay

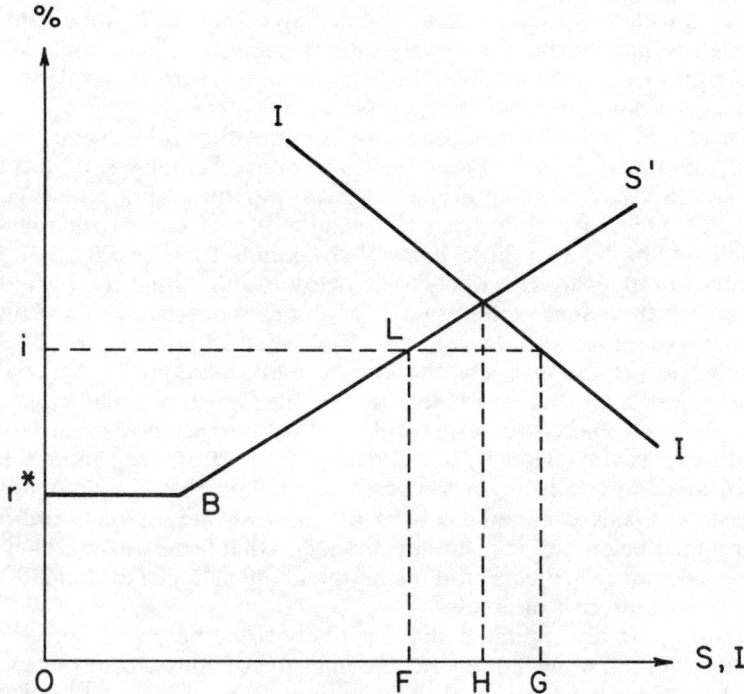

Figure 5.3

for the new assets with corporate savings, i.e. funds that could have been distributed as wages.

In Stephen's diagram, i is drawn *above* r^*, as shown in my Figure 5.3, and he argues that the logic of using the 'cheapest source first' requires that the firm self-finance OF dollars of investment.[4] To borrow those dollars at rate i would be to sacrifice unnecessarily value equal to the area r^*BLi. If after funding OF there remain investment projects with rates of return greater than i, only then will the firm borrow to finance investment. That is, if the marginal efficiency of investment curve II intersects the supply of corporate savings curve to the right of point L, credit will be used to finance additional investment in the firm. Investment will be extended beyond F as long as the cost of funds is less than the return on those funds. As drawn in Figure 5.3, this will be from F out to G. As long as alternative financing for the projects included in distance FG is available at rate i, the workers will not choose to finance them themselves. To do so would be to use retained earnings to save the firm the cost of financing. But having already supplied amount OF, workers will view i (the benefit of not borrowing) as being not high enough to induce them to supply more savings.

If credit were not available, the firm would use corporate savings to finance investment in the amount OH.

Furubotn originally proposed a rigid credit-first rule, arguing that this would lead to more investment and hence higher wages, but he later (1980b) admits that Stephen's cheapest-source-first rule is correct. To Stephen's claim that the availability of credit will reduce self-financing by very little if at all (by amount FH in Figure 5.3), Furubotn replies that i is likely to be below r^*, not above it. He points out that with savings accounts paying 5 per cent or 8 per cent and time horizons of ten years or less, r^* will be between 13 per cent and 25 per cent while the interest rate charged on bank loans in Yugoslavia is usually less than that. If i is less than r^* in Figure 5.3, the firm will follow the cheapest-source-first rule and will finance investment with credit exclusively. That is, it will supply none of its own money for investment in the firm. In that case it appears that the amount of investment is determined solely by the interest rate on loans and the marginal efficiency of investment curve, and that firms will continue to undertake more projects until the marginal efficiency of capital falls to the rate of interest on loans.

To support his argument that i is likely to be below r^*, Furubotn points out that, if the lending rate i equals the savings account rate s, it must necessarily be below r^*. This follows from the fact that for any finite time horizon T, r^* is greater than s. Thus the only way i could be above r^* (and hence some self-financing take place) is if i is above s, substantially so unless T is very large. Thus no self-financing could be expected in a system that relies on a single savings/lending rate to clear the loanable funds market. Instead, whatever investment is undertaken will be financed with borrowed money.

Before turning to the third part of this chapter, where we consider the connection between divisionalization and this reliance on borrowed money, it is important to make clear what Furubotn means by the elimination of self-financing. He is referring to the flow of funds from workers *directly* to their own firms. Because of the Furubotn/Pejovich bias, they will instead prefer to put earnings in individual savings accounts and then have their firms borrow, thus using banks as intermediaries between them and their firms. A consequence of this, he says (1980b, p. 803), is that 'workers will find it harder to see the connection between personal saving and the progress of their own firm. Saving will not seem to be a necessary precondition to capital formation and jobs.'

Internal Banks

But suppose that *within* the firm there were created a 'bank' at which workers could maintain savings accounts. Like ordinary individual accounts, these would pay a fixed rate of interest and the principal could be withdrawn. The only difference from any other Yugoslav bank would be that this bank would lend only to the firm to which it is attached. This arrangement would circumvent the Furubotn/Pejovich bias in that it allows workers to invest in their own firm while retaining limited ownership over their investment: they would not have the control rights of a capitalist entrepreneur (democratic one-worker–one-vote decision-making could continue) but they would have the right to reclaim their money. The bank would perform on the scale of the enterprise one of the major functions of banks in general: it would relieve the problem of the discrepancy between workers' (limited) time horizon and the firm's (unlimited) time horizon, by allowing individuals to take turns serving as creditors while remaining free to cease doing so at any time by withdrawing their funds. There would still be an intermediary between the borrower and the lender, but the process would be much more direct in that savers would know that their money was going to their own firm rather than into the much broader aggregate social capital accumulation.

It might be argued that individual accounts at internal banks would constitute a fundamental change in the principles of the Yugoslav economic system, but I do not agree. As long as the invested capital carries no control rights, the system remains thoroughly worker-managed. All that is changed is that, because workers can recover invested principal, the bias against self-finance is removed. To the extent that the firm were to rely on such a method of financing, it would resemble the Mondragon system, where co-op members temporarily provide capital that they can later reclaim. In Mondragon, however, the system of individual accounts is more rigid: a substantial initial deposit is required when a member joins the firm and withdrawals are not allowed until retirement, at which time he gets the accumulated value, including interest and dividends, of his proportional ownership. If accounts at Yugoslav internal banks were to pay a market rate of interest, as do the Mondragon accounts, this system would satisfy Vanek's major concern (1971) about the financing of labor-managed enterprises: that the absence of a scarcity price for capital leads to inefficient investment decisions.

Furthermore, there are precedents for this concept in Yugoslavia. Both Crvena Zastava, the country's largest automobile producer, and the Yugoslav railway system have sold bonds to raise money. In both cases the public (not necessarily the firm's own workers) loaned money directly to a firm in return for a fixed rate of interest plus some additional benefit (priority on the waiting list for a car or reduced fares for railway travel). This is not so different from putting money in a savings account in return for fixed interest plus the knowledge that one is helping one's own firm's future profits.

A similar notion is found in article 91 of the Law on Associated Labor. This article specifies that a citizen may lend money directly to an enterprise. In fact, it goes further and states that if the loan enables the firm to create additional employment opportunities it may promise the lender a job. In any case, the lender has a right to the return of his money with interest. There have been some cases where this mechanism for 'buying a job' has actually been implemented (*Ekonomska Politika*, 24 October, 1977, pp. 24–6; *Dagens Nyheter* (Stockholm), 3 April, 1978, p. 12; Doder, 1978, p. 88; *Bulletin*, 10 February, 1981, p. 2).

Many large enterprises in Yugoslavia do in fact have internal banks. Some have existed for quite some time but the practice has become much more widespread with the specific encouragement of the Law on Associated Labor. So far they have served only to facilitate the transfer of funds between divisions of a firm (loans as well as transfer payments); but since internal banks already exist, it would not be difficult to create worker savings accounts.

Surprisingly, the creation of such savings accounts would not have much effect on the distribution of risk. Furubotn argues (1980b, p. 803) that, with outside credit, workers 'seem to have the best of both worlds; they can share in any residual their firm makes and, at the same time, avoid sacrificing consumption or risking their own funds in non-owned investment'. Indeed, banks do serve as a buffer between savers and investment projects: whether or not it is at an internal bank, if an account pays a fixed rate of interest the depositors do not bear the entrepreneurial risk of capital suppliers. But this does not mean they avoid risk entirely. They merely bear the risk under a different label. It is well known that, from the point of view of the capitalist firm, raising funds with debt is in one respect *more* risky than raising funds through new equity because of the greater leverage. That is, when funds are borrowed at a fixed interest rate, there is no sharing of the variability of return. Except for the possibility of default, the lender bears none of the risk. When a labor-managed firm borrows at a fixed rate, the workers bear all of the risk of profit uncertainty in that only their incomes are subject to variation. If they lend their own money directly to the firm they may bear part of the risk in their capacity as capital suppliers. In either case the amount of risk is the same and the people who bear it are the same. Where risk sharing does enter is when the firm borrows from outside with an agreement of variable return. If the amount paid to an outside lender is determined by the success of the investment project, then the range of variation of income for the workers is narrowed.

By making clear to workers the connection between saving and the growth of their firm, the internal bank would provide a partial response to Furubotn's concern (1974, p. 275) that 'to workers high consumption and rising incomes appear mutually compatible as long as the firm is able to finance new investment opportunities through the banking system'. However, it would remain true that, in the Yugoslav environment, 'voluntary savings are more difficult to mobilize'. This is largely a result of the fact that a 'varied array of financial instruments is lacking' (Furubotn, 1980b, p. 803). In particular, the traditional capitalist share of stock cannot be offered. It does seem likely that if fewer types of investment devices are available some potential savings will not be tapped.

Interdivisional Lending

In this part of the chapter I set up a straw man and then knock it down. This method is legitimate in this case because the straw man is quite plausible and could easily be accepted as correct by a reasonable person (including, for some time, the present author). It is a notion worth presenting and correcting.

Most of the theoretical literature assumes that any lending that takes place is done by banks. However, the same logic would apply when the lender is another firm or another division of the same firm. From the point of view of the borrower, who supplies the funds is in most cases irrelevant. Further, the apparent importance of borrowing suggests that divisionalization has significant implications for investment decisions. If Furubotn and Stephen are correct in saying that labor-managed firms will invest more with borrowed money than with their own funds, then perhaps divisionalization, which allows the firm to lend to itself, will stimulate investment.

Consider a firm with 3,000 workers. The Furubotn/Pejovich bias suggests that the workers will tend, on marginal decisions, to vote against reinvestment of profit, preferring instead to distribute profit to themselves, put money in savings accounts and then borrow it back from the bank. It is important to remember that this bias is ultimately traceable to their obligation to maintain the investment perpetually. Now suppose this firm organizes itself into ten divisions of 300 workers each. Then any particular project can be treated by 2,700 workers (i.e. nine of the divisions) as though they were outsiders, that is, without obligation to maintain the investment. They can lend money (perhaps 100 per cent of the cost) to the division that technically will own the new assets and then over an agreed period of time they can receive repayment of principal as well as interest. From the point of view of the 300 workers in the other division, the project is being financed by outside credit. Whether that credit comes from a bank or other divisions of the same firm is of no consequence to them. For other investment projects, the divisions could take turns playing banker to one another.

Consider the extreme case of a two-person firm. Suppose the rate paid on savings accounts is 5 per cent and they have a ten-year time horizon, making r^*, the critical rate, 13 per cent. Projects that earn a rate of return greater than 13 per cent will be funded from retained earnings or the workers' own savings, if outside loans are not available. Projects that earn 5–13 per cent will not be funded unless outside credit is available. However, if they 'divisionlize' so that each worker can lend to the other, the following could occur: worker 1 lends $1,000 to worker 2 who uses the money to buy a machine that earns $100 per year net of depreciation. Worker 2 pays off the loan, returning principal plus interest at the rate of 9 per cent, which is more than worker 1 could have earned in a savings account. Worker 1 has no obligation to maintain the assets of the other 'division' and worker 2 is earning 10 per cent with 'outside' financing that cost him 9 per cent. At the same time, worker 2 could lend money to worker 1 so that he too can buy a machine with 'outside' financing.

This arrangement is equivalent to the creation of a small bank similar to that suggested in the second part of this chapter. It takes deposits only from workers in this firm and lends only to this firm. Such a notion is not entirely hypothetical, since large enterprises in Yugoslavia do have internal banks. Furthermore, the idea of one division lending to another is more than just allowed in Yugoslavia; it is strongly encouraged. At first glance, then, it seems that divisionalization provides a way of circumventing the Furubotn/Pejovich bias.

Unfortunately, upon more careful examination, this turns out not to be true. There are problems from the point of view of both the borrower and the lender.

Limitations on Borrowing
The obligation of the borrowing division to maintain undiminished the value of its capital stock means that once it has undertaken a project, even if it is 100 per cent outside financed, the division is committed to future outlays. In most cases it will base its decisions on the return net of depreciation; that is, the project will pay for itself in the sense that the gross revenue it generates will be sufficient to cover the cost of equipment. If it does not, no firm, capitalist or labor-managed, would undertake it. But depreciation can be thought of as either (1) paying

Investment Decisions in the Divisionalized Firm 91

off the loan that financed the initial purchase of the equipment, or (2) being set aside to be used to buy replacement equipment when the original equipment wears out. But, unless double depreciation is subtracted from gross revenue during the life of the original equipment, it will not cover *both* the first and second generations of capital costs. Either depreciation is used to pay off the loan, in which case the division will have to use its own funds to buy the replacement equipment; or depreciation is set aside to buy the replacement equipment, in which case the division uses its own funds to pay off the loan. Either way, the decision to invest, *even with outside financing*, necessarily requires the division to expend its own funds. This expenditure is in addition to the amount conventionally deducted from gross revenue and called depreciation. A capitalist firm, on the other hand, always has the option of not going on to a next generation when the current equipment wears out. It therefore can allocate depreciation to pay off an initial loan. While the Yugoslav firm is not permanently committed to any specific project, once it undertakes some investment it is obligated to continue either that project or other project(s) of equal financial magnitude, and thus it must pay for either the first or second generation of equipment out of its own *net* income, i.e. with money that might otherwise be used for consumption.

Thus there are two related but conceptually distinguishable concepts that must be kept in mind when discussing investment (and borrowing) decisions by the Yugoslav firm: (1) workers cannot regain the principal amount invested, either during the project or at the end; (2) once a decision is made to invest, this necessarily implies a commitment to make future outlays. In order to understand the behavior of the firm, it is not sufficient merely to recognize the practice normally followed of providing for future outlays by setting aside depreciation allowances from the gross return on the project. In explaining the firm's or division's attitude toward borrowing to finance investment, there is more to it than simply looking at the net rather than the gross rate of return on the investment.

Consider again the division discussed above, which has an opportunity to borrow, at 9 per cent interest, the full cost of a machine that will earn a net rate of return of 10 per cent. Should it do so? If the machine lasts forever and the principal amount of the loan may be kept indefinitely (only interest payments being required), the answer is yes; there would be an annual net inflow into the division's wage fund of 1 per cent of the cost of the machine. But if the principal of the loan must be repaid, the answer is not so clear. It may be that the period of repayment is longer than the time horizon of the workers, in which case, although not perpetual, it may be long enough so that they see the burden as falling on the shoulders of future workers. Thus even a 1 per cent interest rate differential may be sufficient to induce them to take the loan and undertake the project. However, if the period of repayment on the loan is shorter than their time horizon, they should realize that the cost of the machine is coming out of their own money and the project should be undertaken only if the rate of return approaches the critical rate r^*. The situation is not that proposed by Vanek (1977, pp. 186–98) where capital is permanently financed and owned by an outside agency. Rather the loan merely allows some postponement of the time when they must themselves pay the money. The important point is that they cannot expect the machine to pay for itself: depreciation allowances are set aside to pay for the machine's replacement. In this respect the Yugoslav firm is different from the capitalist firm because the latter, not being obligated to continue the project (or an equivalent one) when the first machine wears out, has the option of using depreciation allowances to pay off the original loan. This is not to say that an opportunity to borrow is not worth something to the Yugoslav firm; paying later is better than paying sooner. But the point is that the rate of return required to induce workers to invest in owned assets with borrowed money depends on the relationship between the workers' time horizon and the repayment period of the loan. If the period of the loan is short, the rate of return on the investment must be nearly as high as the workers would require to induce them to use their own funds.

A similar circumstance can be found in a capitalist economy. Consider a situation where subsidized loans are available (say, for solar water heaters) at 6 per cent interest. Assuming zero depreciation (the equipment lasts forever), should an individual capitalist take the loan and buy the equipment if it promises to earn 7 per cent? If he had to make only interest payments and could keep the principal indefinitely the answer would be yes. Or if after some period of time he could sell the equipment and pay off the principal in one lump sum, the answer would be yes. But if he must pay off the principal during his own time horizon *and* must keep the equipment (perhaps there is no market for used equipment), then it is a wise investment only if the return on the investment approaches his opportunity cost. If he has other opportunities to invest, say at 10 per cent, it may not be wise to borrow at 6 per cent in order to earn 7 per cent, because eventually it will be *his* money that is tied up at 7 per cent. To be more specific, he should weigh the gain that comes from the 7 per cent minus 6 per cent differential against the loss that he will bear because of the 10 per cent minus 7 per cent differential. Obviously, the length of time for each is crucial.

The fact that the relationship between the period of the loan and the workers' time horizon is important in their decision about borrowing is pointed out by Stephen (1978, pp. 228, 230, 234, 236). He claims that the minimum return necessary to induce them to borrow (which he calls the 'effective burden' of the loan) is found by adjusting the interest rate on the loan using the same formula used to calculate r. For example, if the interest rate on savings accounts is 5 per cent and workers' time horizon is ten years, expression (3) tells us that the equivalent return on self-financed investment projects in the firm is 12.95 per cent. Suppose also that loans are available at 8 per cent. Stephen applies expression (3) to the 8 per cent figure and concludes that a return of at least 14.90 per cent would be needed to induce workers to use credit.

He bases this rather surprising result on the fact that if they use credit the workers will have to pay not only (eventually) the principal cost of the project, but also the cost of servicing a loan (i.e. the interest). Now, if the loan is to be repaid very soon (say, within a year), then an expected return on the project of just slightly more than 12.95 per cent will be sufficient to induce the workers to undertake the investment. But if the loan is to be outstanding for longer, then the total cost of servicing will be higher and hence the expected return must be higher. The 14.90 per cent above is the required return if the loan period exactly equals the workers' time horizon. Stephen shows the formula to be

$$r = \left[\frac{(1+i)^J - 1}{i(1+i)^J} + \frac{(1+s)^T - 1}{s(1+s)^T} - \frac{(1+s)^J - 1}{s(1+s)^J} \right]^{-1}$$

where

i = the interest rate on loans
J = the length of the loan period
s = the interest rate earned on savings accounts
T = the workers' time horizon

This formula is based on the assumption that the principal is repaid in a single final payment in period J.

If the loan period exceeds the time horizon, then the required return depends on the specific repayment schedule. If the principal is to be repaid in a single final lump-sum payment, then a loan period greater than the workers' time horizon is tantamount to not repaying the principal at all. In that case any project whose return exceeds the borrowing rate will be undertaken (in this case anything over 8 per cent). If the principal is to be repaid in installments over the life of the loan, then a longer loan period means smaller principal payments during the time horizon and hence a *lower* rate of return would be required. Thus, for a given time horizon, the required rate of return increases as the loan period increases from very short up to the workers' time horizon, and then decreases as the loan period exceeds that time horizon by more and more.

An implication of this analysis is that both Furubotn and Stephen are wrong in claiming that with credit available at rate i the Yugoslav firm will invest out to amount G in Figure 5.3. Indeed, it is true that beyond amount F they would prefer to borrow rather than use corporate savings; but a loan at interest rate i that must be repaid in a few weeks will not induce them to invest beyond point H, because after those few weeks it will be their own money tied up in the project. Depending on the relationship between their time horizon and the period of the loan, they will invest out to some point between H and G. Even if i is below r^*, it remains true that the amount of investment undertaken will be somewhere between H and the intersection of i and the II curve, depending on the duration of loans. The greater the amount by which the loan period exceeds the time horizon, the smaller will be the amount of principal the workers will pay off (or take over) during their time horizon, and hence the more willing they will be to borrow in order to undertake projects they would not be willing to finance entirely by themselves.

Having just argued that workers may not borrow in circumstances where Furubotn expects them to, I now want to point out that they may borrow in cases where he expects them not to. Furubotn argues (1980a, p. 187, equation (2)), that a project must promise a rate of return at least equal to r in order to warrant borrowing at rate i. That return allows the firm to pay off the original loan in τ time periods in addition to setting aside appropriate depreciation allowances. It is then left with a self-financing project that gives a perpetual return. Furubotn says that a rate of return less than r is not sufficient to induce the investment, but that may not be true. If at rate of return r the net into-workers'-pockets cash flow is zero (1980a, p. 186, iii) during the loan period, then after τ periods it is zero *plus* the amount of the principal and interest payments that no longer need be paid to the lender. If the return were a little lower than r, the firm would have a negative net cash flow during τ periods, but it still might have a positive cash flow after the loan is paid off. Clearly, the workers might be willing to do it. Elsewhere Furubotn himself specifically mentions the possibility that 'consumption is shifted forward from one time period to another' (1974, p. 262). But the two-period model he uses there cannot reflect benefits that persist *after* the loan is paid off. This consideration is crucial if the loan period is shorter than the workers' time horizon.

Limitations on Lending

If we are to understand the effect of the divisionalization on the firm's investment behavior, we must also look at the situation from the lender's point of view. First of all, as the loan is repaid, not all of the money can be used by the lender for consumption. Until 1968, both the principal and interest of loan repayments had to go into the lending firm's or division's business fund. Since 1969, interest earned on interfirm and interdivision loans may legally be distributed for individual consumption, but of course the principal may not.[5] In the example cited earlier, worker 1 may consume the interest on the loan to worker 2, but as the $1,000 principal is paid off it must go into his business fund. Thus any money that workers lend to a sister division is as permanently out of reach for consumption purposes as money used to purchase assets for their own division.

It is also important to recognize that most discussions of investment in the Yugoslav firm assume a fundamental dichotomy: funds come either from external loans or from internal sources (retained earnings) that would otherwise be distributed as wages. It might be useful to distinguish between two types of internal funds: the business fund and additional voluntary savings. The former is a fund that accumulates depreciation payments made against the wearing out of machinery purchased at some earlier time. The latter is money that has been or could be paid out to workers. Since voluntary savings, once loaned to another division, are no more available for consumption than money used to buy assets for their own division, workers will lend those savings only if the expected return is higher than what can be earned in their own division and only if the rate of return is greater than r. But what about depreciation funds, which are not available for personal consumption anyway? Will divisions lend to one another their accumulated depreciation funds?

Returning again to the two-person firm that 'divisionalizes', suppose each division used its half of the enterprise's business fund to finance the other's new machine. Thus two new machines are bought using internal funds. Now each begins to repay the other's business fund for the cost of the machine, plus interest on the loan. Also, each will begin to pay into its own divisional business fund annual depreciation on its new machine. Eventually *each* divisional business fund will accumulate loan payments and depreciation totalling the price of *two* machines. That is, for the firm as a whole, the total amount of money paid into the business funds (and thus unavailable for consumption) will be twice as much as would have been paid in had each division paid for its own machine or had the firm not divisionalized.

This result is not difficult to explain. The business fund initially holds a sum of money accumulated by earlier depreciation payments (paid against the wearing out of older machines). These funds can be used by the firm to buy new machines without any obligation to repay, other than the depreciation payments that eventually will replace the *new* machine. But if the money is divided in half and *loaned* by one division to the other, then the new machines are not considered to be replacements for earlier machines; hence the loans must be repaid *in addition* to the depreciation payments that each division must make into its own fund. This boils down to saying that it makes more sense to use funds that do not need to be repaid than funds that do.

Of course, these limitations on borrowing and lending do not mean that divisions will never borrow from one another. There will be times when a division wants to invest more than its current accumulation of depreciation payments; if the division has already supplied as much of its own savings as it is willing to, given the expected return, then it will seek a loan. At the same time, there may be another division that has accumulated funds that it does not plan to use immediately. Depending on the length of time the funds will be tied up, the latter may be willing to provide the outside credit sought by the former. But clearly, the borrower is borrowing only because it has not accumulated enough depreciation funds.

If the borrower is seeking a loan at all, it is because it prefers not to pay for the project with additional voluntary savings; therefore, it will prefer the longest repayment period it can get, so as to delay contributing its own money. Consequently, the time period on an interdivisional loan will depend on the lender's current and expected alternative investment opportunities. Since depreciation funds may not be consumed, they are valuable only if they are put to work, either by converting them to physical assets within the division or by lending them to someone. Then the earnings on the investment may be distributed and consumed. Therefore, the lending division will agree to whatever period of time it expects before a more attractive use for the money will come along. That is, it must consider the likely timing of investment opportunities within its own division as well as the anticipated rates of return on its own projects and those in other divisions.

Obviously, a division will not lend to another unless the return is at least as high as the interest paid by banks on corporate deposits. Officially, the rate of interest on loans between firms or divisions is limited to 10 per cent, but if both parties agree it is often quite easy to make the effective return higher by including in the arrangement transfer prices that are favorable to the lender. There may also be other benefits to the lender, such as increased availability or improved quality of some input to its own production process. Thus it may accept from a sister division a rate of interest that is nominally lower than the bank rate. In cases where the return is not a fixed percentage, but varies with the success of a project, the lender must calculate an expected return and probably will require a premium for uncertainty.

In considering the rate of interest necessary to induce a division to lend to another division, the following should be kept in mind: a decision to buy assets for their own division not only makes money unavailable for consumption, but creates an obligation to buy more assets at some future time when these wear out, whereas a decision to lend to another division means money will be returned with no further obligations on the part of the lender. That is, when considering an investment in real assets, a division must look at the return net of the depreciation that must be set aside for future replacement; when considering a loan to another division, the relevant return is the gross rate of interest because no commitment is made for future outlays. In other words, investment in a financial instrument, as opposed to a physical asset, involves no depreciation.

The borrower, on the other hand, can offer to pay no more than the *net* rate of return on the proposed project because it must set aside depreciation allowances for eventual replacement of the asset. The rate actually paid on interdivisional loans will result from negotiations between borrower and lender. But it must be somewhere between the lender's opportunity cost and the borrower's net return on the project being financed.

Summary

The purpose of this chapter has been to investigate some topics relating to investment decisions in order to understand better the case studies of corporate structure that appear in the next chapter.

The theoretical literature suggests that there is a bias that dissuades workers from investing in their own firms. On the other hand, inflation may produce an opposite bias. If the inflation bias less than fully offsets the other, then the amount of investment a firm will undertake may depend heavily on the availability of outside credit. If this is true and if each division of a firm treats loans from other divisions as outside credit, then one might expect more investment when the firm is divisionalized. That is, lending divisions would treat loans as interest-earning investments that are not subject to depreciation payments, and borrowing divisions would undertake projects they would not finance themselves. However, careful analysis shows that there are obstacles on both the borrowing and lending sides.

Whether or not Yugoslav firms or divisions will invest more with borrowed money than with their own savings depends entirely on the length of time of the loan relative to their time horizon. A loan that must be repaid very quickly will not induce workers to undertake a project they would otherwise reject. A loan that can be repaid at some time beyond the workers' time horizon may do so. We cannot generalize about the duration of a loan from another division because it depends on the lender's expectations about alternative opportunities. Such loans could be quite short-term.

In an economic system where investment in physical capital carries significant commitments and the range of financial instruments is severely limited, we might expect potential lenders to be anxious to invest in a way that does not obligate them to make future outlays. A loan to a sister division will be treated as a project that has a zero rate of depreciation: it does not require additional annual outlays. However, the funds involved are not more available for consumption (in the present or future) than funds invested directly in physical capital: in either case the interest but not the principal may be used for consumption. It is therefore money already in the division's business fund that it might be willing to lend, not additional voluntary savings beyond what the workers would be willing to invest in their own division. Only some system of internal individual savings accounts would elicit further individual contributions.

On the other hand, the higher the rate of inflation, the more anxious a division will be to transform financial assets into real assets. If it sees no prospect of a more productive use within its own division, a potential lender may well choose to invest in another division. Whether the most attractive opportunities are in divisions in the same or other enterprises is in many respects unimportant.

Further, the extent to which the lender shares in the risks of a new project depends on the type of loan: if a fixed rate of return is promised, there is only the danger of default, but if the agreement specifies a profit share then the lender's realized return will vary with the success of the project.

Notes

1 In some of his articles Furubotn specifically requires that earnings be fully paid out each period, and yet he does not relate this to the question of the rate at which they compound until time T. See Furubotn (1974), pp. 267–72; (1976), p. 116; (1980b), p. 801. For discussion of the appropriate rate of discount for labor-managed firms, see Steinherr and Peer (1975) and Atkinson (1975).
2 Pejovich (1973, p. 29) admits that rising prices may affect the choice between savings accounts and other individual investments, but he does not recognize the effect of inflation on the choice between individual and collective investment. We might note that the alternatives he suggests (land, gold and foreign currencies) are not realistic options for most Yugoslav citizens.

3 While the annual return is in the form of real goods and services and hence is indexed for inflation, the subsequent compounding will occur in workers' savings accounts, which are not immune to inflation. Hence the inflation-based bias toward investment in the firm is not quite as strong as indicated.
4 As a homely analogy, I might point out that for purchases already made (or definitely decided upon), a wise consumer should not use a credit card that incurs a 16 per cent finance charge if he can pay with funds in or destined for a savings account that earns 8 per cent (setting aside questions of self-discipline or preferences for liquidity).
5 Article 8 of the 1968 Fundamental Law on the Determination and Distribution of Income in Work Organizations (*Službeni List*, No. 32, 7 August, 1968) states that the total revenue of a work organization includes, 'in addition to the value of goods sold and services provided . . . all other revenues realized in its business: revenue on the basis of agreements on joining assets for joint business, revenue from interest on loaned assets, . . .'. See Sirc (1979), p. 130; Furubotn and Pejovich (1970), p. 241; and Vacić (1978), p. 19.

6 Case Studies

In the course of writing this book I have studied, in varying degrees of detail, thirty-seven large Yugoslav corporations, including twenty-four that I visited personally. In order to shed light on the nature and functioning of Yugoslav enterprises, this chapter examines in detail actual relationships between and within some of these firms.

Most of the chapter is devoted to presenting the specific arrangements at five firms. The first case is based on a self-management agreement that I obtained directly from the firm itself. The next four cases discussed are taken from a book titled *Principi i Politika Dohotka* ('Principles and Policies of Income') by Aleksandar M. Vacić (1980), who, in his capacity as vice president of the Belgrade Komora,[1] was intimately involved in drawing up these agreements. After that I look briefly at the 'KLEK' enterprises described by Comisso (1979, 1980) and at some of the eight firms described by Zapp (1983).

It is not possible to be certain that these cases are representative of common Yugoslav industrial organization practice. There is always a possibility that any particular set of examples is somehow atypical. Some observers might argue that these are normative, that is, examples of how things are *supposed* to work. However, as someone who has over a number of years visited dozens of Yugoslav firms, talked to many economists (both Yugoslav and American), and read extensively on this topic, I believe that these are not inconsistent with how such things work in Yugoslavia. Further, if divisions of enterprises do have substantial autonomy (and I believe they do), then they certainly need some sort of mechanism to coordinate their various activities, especially investment: the arrangements evident in these cases are not only those prescribed by law, they are the only ones widely discussed. It is very unlikely that procedures that are typical would not be thoroughly discussed.

In most of this chapter attention is focused on joint investment, but I do not mean to suggest that all investment is handled jointly; there is, of course, a good deal of investment undertaken by a single division. But that activity is not the subject of this book. Also, it should be pointed out at the very outset that in principle the parties to any contract are supposed to be divisions, not enterprises. That means that the distinction between intrafirm and interfirm relationships is not clear. It is usually true that relationships between divisions in separate firms are different from the relationships between divisions in the same firm. But in some cases divisions that are nominally in separate enterprises form bonds that essentially constitute a merger: they create a relationship that reduces opportunistic behavior and is built on what amounts to a sharing clause. That is, they establish an income-sharing agreement and a mechanism for decision-making that allows the adaptive, sequential decision-making that is characteristic of firms. This occurs even though they do not formally merge in the sense of adopting a common name and a single administrative hierarchy. In Yugoslavia, even the most cohesive enterprises have multiple administrative hierarchies.

In reading these cases one frequently finds oneself asking two questions: is this an agreement between firms or within a single firm? do transfer prices really affect the allocation of resources or do they merely serve to distribute income? Often Yugoslav industrial organization defies simple answers to these questions. While several of the cases examined in this chapter each involve more than one enterprise, they are essentially interdivisional (although not intrafirm) agreements. In those cases it is difficult to give clear-cut answers to these two questions; but most do include some features that support the notion that they have formed a single firm. In at least three of the first five cases in this chapter there are grounds for arguing that transfer prices do affect the allocation of resources, and that argument is at least plausible in the Comisso and Zapp cases. As I showed in chapter 1, this holds even where the dominant mechanism appears to be the dividing up of revenue from the sale of a final product. All of these cases can best be understood as a set of internal contracts.

Varteks

Varteks (Varaždinski Tekstilni Kombinat) is a textile firm that I visited at its headquarters in Varaždin, which is about 60 kilometers north of Zagreb. In 1977, Varteks ranked 79th on *Ekonomska Politika*'s list of the largest Yugoslav industrial enterprises. It employed 8,947 workers and earned total revenue of 3.44 billion dinars (approximately $191 million). Its total assets were valued then at 2.59 billion dinars (approximately $144 million).

Like many large Yugoslav firms, Varteks grew out of a long tradition and an old factory. The area around Varaždin has been active in textile manufacturing for 400 years, and the firm itself traces its history to a mill started in 1902 to make cotton yarn and fabric. It later added woolen fabrics to its activities and since 1962 has produced a wide range of clothing. It also makes a variety of synthetics and recently added automobile brake linings.

The wide range of activities carried out within the enterprise is evident from the organizational chart shown in Table 6.1. In addition to the obvious production activities, the firm supplies workers with hot meals and medical care, builds apartments (about 1,000 since 1947),

Table 6.1 *Divisional Structure of Varteks*

Work Organization for the Production of Yarn and Cloth

    Yarn Division
    Cloth Division
    Novi Marof[a] Division
    Work Community for Joint Services

Work Organization for the Production of Clothing

    Unit I Division
    Unit II Division
    Ludbreg[a] Division
    Ivanec[a] Division
    Bednja[a] Division
    Health Care Division
    Work Community for Joint Services

Work Organization for Technical Help Activities

    Thermoenergy Division
    Electrical Energy Division
    Machine Repair Division
    Construction Division

Vartimpeks (import–export) Division

Social Standard (cafeteria) Division

Transportation Division

Retail Trade Division (186 shops including 4 large department stores)

Printing Division

Machine Building Division

Work Community for Joint Services[b]

---

[a] Novi Marof, Ludbreg, Ivanec and Bednja are towns within 30 kilometers of Varaždin.
[b] Includes engineering, personnel, bookkeeping, finance, legal services, security, fire protection, etc.

operates vacation resorts at the seacoast and provides workers with transportation to and from work.

A glance at the organizational chart shows that the structural relationships among divisions (basic organizations of associated labor, or BOALs) and work organizations (*radna organizacija* or *zajednica osnovna organizacija*, which means community of basic organizations) are not consistent. Some, but not all, divisions are part of a work organization. Those divisions that are not part of work organizations are in some cases, but not always, treated as parallel to the work organizations. For example, of the eight structural units contributing to the cost of economic planning, three are work organizations and five are divisions.

The 'Self-Management Agreement on the Fundamentals of the 1977 Plan' reveals a good deal about Varteks. The document is intended to implement the firm's basic self-management agreement. It specifies the obligations of each subunit of the firm – joint investment, incomes policy, financing of joint services, etc. Specific output targets are given for each unit and complete financial accounts are spelled out in considerable detail. The document is approved by the *enterprise* executive board but is not valid until accepted and signed by two-thirds of the divisions and work communities.

Article 7 of the planning agreement cites the firm's basic self-management agreement to support the notion that 'the price of goods and services in internal trade is in principle the market price'. The relationship among the divisions within the firm is very much influenced by the fact that, in addition to the transactions that occur within the firm, many divisions also buy and sell outside the firm. Only 50 per cent of the fabric they make is further processed within the enterprise and nearly 50 per cent of the fabric they use to make clothing comes from outside. Furthermore, while they are the largest woolen textile firm in Yugoslavia, they still account for only 9 per cent of total domestic yarn production, 8 per cent of domestic cloth production and 4 per cent of clothing. That means that, if internal intermediate goods prices exceed market prices, the final goods cannot compete on the domestic market.

Appendix 4 of the agreement sets out internal prices with considerable precision. This includes prices for steam and electricity, hourly rates for electricians and repairmen, hourly and distance rates for transportation (broken down by type of truck: a Mercedes 5-ton costs 8.3 dinars per kilometer and a TAM 2-ton costs 5.1 dinars per kilometer), meals from the cafeteria division (each worker pays 3 dinars and his division pays a subsidy of an addition 10.8 dinars), and services of the export division (0.5 per cent of the value of the goods exported).

Goods and services for which there is no external market are priced by internal negotiations. These negotiations are taken very seriously and consume a good deal of time. One of the functions of the central office is to serve as arbitrator. Article 35 states that 'it is agreed that joint services are compensated on the basis of their contributions, i.e. the calculated value of their services to the participants [division]'. Using these prices and the extent to which each work organization and basic organization is expected to use the various services, it is possible to calculate the exact financial flows. Appendix 13 shows, down to the last dinar, the amount that each user will pay for each of the services, such as bookkeeping, personnel, finance, etc. For some services, like the headquarters office staff, union activities and health care, each division pays in proportion to the number of its employees. If the income of the divisions is greater or less than planned, their payments for some joint services increases or decreases according to agreed criteria (article 36).

Article 47 lays out a set of rules for internal trade. Considerable attention is paid to meeting scheduled delivery dates (seasonal changes are very important in the textile and clothing industry). For example, delivery between eight and fifteen days late results in a penalty of 5 per cent of the value of the shipment; lateness of fifteen–thirty days means a penalty of 10 per cent; failure to deliver by the thirtieth day after the scheduled time means a 15 per cent fine. After fifteen days late, the buying division has the right to cancel the order and to take the 10 or 15 per cent penalty for damages.

Article 47 also states that a seller cannot sell outside the firm at lower prices or more favorable conditions. If it sells outside the firm anything promised to be exclusively available inside, the seller must give the inside buyer a 10 per cent discount. If an inside buyer refuses to accept delivery of goods that meet agreed standards, he must pay damages of 20 per cent of the value of the shipment.

If a division has an opportunity to buy outside at a particularly favorable price, it can do so as long as it does not cancel on short notice a commitment inside. For example, a clothing division took advantage of a one-time chance to ship some goods at particularly low freight rates. However, in most cases the internal price for transportation is lower than the outside price because the former covers only current costs: replacement and expansion of capital in the transportation and retail trade divisions are funded directly by the production organizations. In machine repair and construction, on the other hand, instances of dealing outside are quite common. Not only do Varteks divisions buy repair and construction services from other firms, but the Varteks divisions sell these services outside as well.

Varteks retail shops sell clothing produced by other firms but only under certain conditions: they must be made of cloth bought from

Varteks and they must not be exactly comparable to Varteks products. That is, they are used to fill out the assortment produced by the firm.

An interesting aspect of the plan document is that it both explicitly emphasizes the need to reduce the labor force by eliminating some jobs (article 17) and at the same time states that employment security is guaranteed (article 18). The two are reconciled by relying on retirement and retraining. When someone retires, his job is to be either eliminated or filled by someone from elsewhere in the enterprise. Retraining is paid for by enterprise headquarters and the salary during the training period is paid by the division or work community where the worker was previously employed.

Much of this document is taken up with specification of amounts of money to be set aside for special purposes and details of which units will contribute how much for each purpose. The expenditures include costs of drawing up this planning document, education (courses, training, seminar, etc.), gifts to retiring workers, collective consumption, advertising, health care and cultural events. While some costs are allocated on the basis of number of workers, others, for example advertising, fall primarily on the production divisions.

All financial flows are handled through the internal bank (*zajednica služba za financije*). Each division gives whatever funds it has available to the internal bank, which pays the division 8 per cent interest. Any division in temporary difficulties is to be helped out by the others through the internal bank, under the condition that the borrowing division 'compensate the others, in addition to interest, for what they would have earned by using that money themselves' (article 33). This explicit recognition of the notion of opportunity cost makes good sense except for the phrase 'in addition to interest'. I was told that what they meant was 'the opportunity cost if it is greater than the interest rate'.

BIGZ and MATROZ

In the second case, I examine an agreement that involves two separate enterprises. Like subsequent cases, it shows that many of the mechanisms used to coordinate activities and to distribute income among divisions in separate firms are identical to the mechanisms used to govern the relationships among divisions within a single enterprise.

The case involves Beogradski Izdavačko–Grafički Zavod (BIGZ) and Fabrika Celuloze i Papira Matroz (MATROZ). BIGZ is a publishing and newspaper enterprise and MATROZ manufactures various types of paper, including newsprint and offset paper. The two firms have had a buyer–seller relationship for many years. However, because their needs and abilities had not been closely coordinated,

MATROZ was not always able to fill BIGZ's orders and MATROZ occasionally found itself unable to sell its output. The problem concerned particular types of paper as well as total quantity available.

The situation is complicated by the fact that BIGZ has a division of its own called 'Paper Factory', which, unlike MATROZ, had reasonably good access to supplies of cellulose pulp. At the time of this agreement, cellulose was in particularly short supply domestically, and was increasingly scarce on world markets where demand from new users outside the paper industry was being felt.

The two firms asked Vacić to draw up an agreement that would achieve 'planned and secure' supply of paper for BIGZ and 'secure placement' of its output for MATROZ, while insulating them from the 'oscillations of the marketplace' (Vacić, 1976, p. 371). The essence of the agreement finally reached is that BIGZ and MATROZ will jointly expand the production of cellulose. This will be done by modernizing and expanding the capacity of the cellulose division of MATROZ. BIGZ will contribute money and MATROZ will contribute both labor and money.

An interesting aspect of this case is that Vacić provides us with some early drafts of the agreement that he rejected because they were ambiguous or violate the Constitution. It is very instructive to learn that the corporate laywers who drafted the agreement think in terms of 'profit' (a word not defined in Yugoslav law; 'residual income' should be used instead), 'co-owner' (article 12 of the Constitution says that no one owns social capital), and 'lasting right of ownership' (this violates not only article 12 of the Constitution but also article 26, which prohibits permanent income sharing on the basis of contributed funds).

A possibly important point is that the enterprises as well as the particular divisions are parties to this agreement. It is signed by representatives of each of five entitites: two BIGZ divisions, one MATROZ division and both enterprises. This contrasts with other case studies where only the divisions sign. In this case it is difficult to say whether this is an agreement between enterprises or between divisions only. Vacić says that the enterprise signatures convey a promise that the firm as a whole guarantees fulfillment of all the obligations of its division(s). But there appears to be more to it than that: article 4 states that BIGZ supplies funds, while article 9 states that the two BIGZ *divisions* have a right to a share of the income earned. One could argue that in effect, at least with regard to these transactions, the firms have merged.

This argument is supported by the fact that the agreement calls for creation of a joint business council (despite the fact that BIGZ contributes only capital and no labor). This council can be viewed as a mechanism that makes possible the adaptive, sequential decision-making discussed in chapter 4. In the version originally proposed by MATROZ, BIGZ would get a number of representatives on that council in proportion to its invested capital. Vacić objected that such a principle might give too large a share of control to those who are contributing no current labor. In the final version, the two BIGZ divisions plus the BIGZ enterprise as a whole are each allowed to appoint one delegate, but, surprisingly, the number of MATROZ delegates (and hence the size of the council) is not specified.

For purposes of discussion, the specific details of the agreement can be put into two categories: (1) the buying and selling of goods, and (2) the investment and return of capital. These two aspects of the agreement are explicitly kept separate: article 14 specifies that the goods transactions will continue even after termination of the investment relationship. The buying and selling of goods are fairly simple. BIGZ is committed to buy from MATROZ 5,000 tons of cellulose and 3,000 tons of newsprint and offset paper annually for three years; after that it will increase its purchases to 8,000 tons of cellulose and 5,000 tons of paper annually. Furthermore, BIGZ will sell to MATROZ at least 1,000 tons of pulp annually. The prices of these goods are to be 'the current domestic market prices' (article 7) found by taking the average of prices paid on the Yugoslav market. 'The conditions of payment and other details are those of wholesale trade in general' (Vacić, 1976, p. 373).

The details of the investment and its repayment are also fairly straightforward. BIGZ agrees to invest a total of 30 million dinars (at the time, the equivalent of $1.7 million) to be paid on specified dates during a two-year period of construction. This is a loan, not a permanent investment. Repayment must begin within five years of completion of the construction project. The exact schedule of repayment is left up to MATROZ (more specifically, its cellulose division), but article 8 of the agreement requires that it be fully repaid no later than ten years after the new capacity is in operation.

No explicit interest is paid on the loan. Instead, until the loan is fully paid off, BIGZ has a right to share in the income earned by the cellulose division of MATROZ. Article 11 specifies that this share is determined as follows. From the net income earned by the newly modernized and expanded cellulose division, enough money is deducted to provide its workers with personal income and collective consumption at a level equivalent to that of workers in the two BIGZ divisions that are involved in this deal. The remainder of the net income is to be divided between, on the one hand, the two BIGZ divisions and, on the other hand, the MATROZ cellulose division in proportion to the amount of funds invested by each. That proportion is the ratio of 30 million to x, where x is the sum of the book value of the equipment already in the cellulose division plus any additional investment that MATROZ may make in the project. This income-sharing arrangment can be viewed as the sharing clause, which I argued in chapter 4, allows the participants to rely on incomplete long-term contracts.

One of the most interesting aspects of this arrangement is that the workers in the cellulose division of MATROZ are not entirely residual claimants. In accordance with article 26 of the Constitution and article 82 of the Basic Law on Associated Labor, the agreement requires that funds first be provided for their personal incomes and collective consumption at a level equal to that of workers in the two BIGZ divisions. Only then can any residual be divided up. This reflects a basic difference between this and some of the subsequent cases. In the IMT–IMR case, for example, both firms provide both labor and capital, whereas in this case BIGZ is providing only capital. Hence, what is being divided up is only capital's share. Of course, to say that labor's share in the new project is equal to whatever workers are earning in BIGZ is merely an ad hoc approach without theoretical justification, but it does have the advantages of being easily implemented and of seeming fair.

An early draft of this agreement stated that the funds invested by BIGZ would be returned 'through participation in realized joint income' (article 17 of the first MATROZ version). Vacić reminds us that article 26 of the Constitution gives BIGZ a right to an income share 'in addition to' the return of its investment. Article 85 of the Basic Law on Associated Labor says it may waive that right, but such a waiver must be made explicit in the agreement. In the final version there is no waiver and article 5 specifies that BIGZ gets both income share and the return of its invested funds.

An obvious question is whether BIGZ's share of joint income diminishes as its investment is repaid. This possibility is not mentioned anywhere in the agreement or in Vacić's discussion of it. Clearly if such a diminution were intended it would have to be spelled out, so apparently BIGZ receives a fixed percentage of that joint income right up to the time its funds are fully repaid.

Another point that Vacić objected to is the statement that 'this agreement remains in effect for an indefinite time' (article 12 of the first BIGZ version). Because article 26 of the Constitution prohibits permanent income sharing on the basis of invested funds, some termination must be specified. Consequently the final agreement states that BIGZ's right to share in the joint income lasts only 'as long as the assets which BIGZ contributed are not entirely returned' (article 9).

Vacić also objected to a statement in the first MATROZ version (articles 4 and 17) that it return the nominal amount of BIGZ's funds.

He recommends (1976, p. 379) that there be at least a partial adjustment for inflation, perhaps by using the official revaluation of assets, but the final version does not contain such a provision.

MALI MAKIŠ

The third case involves the construction industry in Belgrade. The industry consists of a large number of firms, many of which are quite small. Many indicators of speed and quality of construction show the industry to be rather inefficient, as do several measures of per-unit cost and income per worker. As we often hear from Yugoslav economists, Vacić suggests that the problem is essentially a matter of excessive fragmentation of firms and the absence of specialization. The answer, he (along with many others) believes, is to draw up agreements that will coordinate the activities of the various firms in the industry. There have been some mergers, but they have not fundamentally improved the situation. What they think is needed is broad coordination and cooperation. The agreements we turn to now are meant to provide a part of that coordination.

One of the many problems facing the industry is a scarcity of cement. Many firms expressed an interest in setting up a new factory, but their needs are so heterogeneous that it was deemed best to draw up first a fundamental agreement to regulate a whole complex of production facilities and then, separately, to conclude several more specific agreements. They settled on Mali Makiš as the location of five production facilities: sand and gravel, cement, fresh concrete, pre-stressed concrete shapes, and elements for prefabricated construction.

Vacić provides us with both the general agreement covering the entire complex and the specific agreement for one of the particular products, fresh concrete, which he says is representative of the five product-specific agreements.

The general agreement covering the whole complex at Mali Makiš consists mostly of rather vague statements of principle. For example, article 6 states:

> Relations between those basic organizations of Mali Makiš between which there is vertical division of labor or other form of created income from joint labor will be regulated on the principles of jointly created income and its distribution among mutually related basic organizations of associated labor, in proportion to the contributions that each of them gives with its total, current and past labor.
>
> On the principles of the previous paragraph will also be formed mutual economic relations between each individual future basic

organization of Mali Makiš, each signatory of this agreement and other interested organizations, if among them there should be vertical division of labor or other similar form of realizing income through joint work and business. [My translation]

The purpose of this agreement is to arrange the creation of Mali Makiš as an enterprise (*radna organizacija*) within which there will be divisions created by other agreements. It does state specific figures for the expected capacity of each of the five divisions, but says that these are only approximate. The individual division agreeements will determine exact output capacity as well as the obligations of each division to the signatories. It is interesting that the agreement refers not only to the divisions' obligation to deliver goods, but also to the obligation of the signatories to purchase the goods.

Article 7 states that in order to build new production capacity, the signatories of the agreement will pool their own funds and will jointly seek credit. The credit will be repaid by the signatories out of money returned to them by the future divisions of Mali Makiš and out of the signatories' share of the income earned by those divisions. Clearly, this article is not sufficiently precise to be operational. More specific arrangements are left for the individual product agreements. Similarly, the prices of goods are to be determined in each agreement.

Also explicitly left to the individual agreements are arrangements for return of the funds invested by the signatories. Until those funds are returned, the signatories have a right to a share of the income earned by the divisions. However, as in the BIGZ–MATROZ case, residual income for distribution is calculated only after subtracting from revenue enough funds for the personal incomes and collective consumption of the workers in each division.

The general agreement calls for creation of a joint council including representatives of the signatories, special interest groups, the city government, banks and the *komora*. There are no worker representatives because at this stage there are not yet any workers.

As an example of the specific agreements that create the divisions within Mali Makiš, Vacić prints the agreement that establishes the fresh concrete division. Seven firms are signatories of this agreement, the purpose of which is to set down some basic rules that will govern the operation of this division. Unlike our previous cases, none of the signatories are themselves divisions: all are enterprises.

Annual production of 150,000 cubic meters of fresh concrete will be sold to outsiders as well as to the signatories of this agreement. The exact quantities and delivery schedules are to be set down in a separate document, which is to be signed at the same time as this agreement. Technically, it is the signatories of this agreement, that is, the founders, who are legally committed to supply concrete to the outsiders; but article 14 states that once the new concrete division is established this obligation is transferred to it and that the obligation to supply concrete continues even after the new division has repaid to the founders the funds they had invested.

In case of shortages, the signatories and those who have agreements with them get priority on deliveries of concrete, at least within the limits set in the agreement. If the shortage is very severe, the signatories get quantities in proportion to the amount of funds they invested in construction of the cement-making facilities. Also, the obligations are reciprocal; that is, the producing division has a guaranteed market because the signatories must buy the agreed quantities.

Article 7 sets the rules for prices: at times when cement is under government price restrictions, the government sets the price; when under partial control, the price will be negotiated; if not controlled, it will equal the average price on the Yugoslav market. Thus prices are not an afterthought, to be determined when the time comes to distribute income; rather they are determined exogenously or negotiated. Decisions about output (even if made infrequently in long-term contracts) are made on the basis of past and expected prices. That is, prices do affect resource allocation.

Funds for the construction of new concrete-making capacity are to be provided by the signatories of the agreement, using both their own money and credit arranged by them. They are responsible for arranging credit in amounts proportional to the amount of their own money that they supply.

An interesting twist to this case is the fact that the signatories are themselves construction firms and hence interested in doing the actual work of constructing the new facilities. Article 4 states that where possible the building work will be done by those firms. There is no statement that such work would be done for free, or that such work would constitute a contribution to the new division, so apparently it would be paid for.

The legal status of the new division is discussed in article 5 of the agreement. During construction it has the status of 'organization under construction' (*organizacija u izgradnji*) and all legal liability is carried jointly by the signatories. Once the new capacity is put into regular production, the division will be officially registered as a basic organization of associated labor. At that point the workers in the division, 'together with the signatories and other organizations', will decide whether the division will operate as an independent enterprise (*radna organizacija*), as a division of one of the signatories, as a division of Mali Makiš, 'or in some other way which is judged best'. No guidance is given as to how this decision will be made. But whatever is decided, the division will be linked with all the signatories by a complex organization of associated labor (*složena organizacija*) as long as the obligations of the agreement are in effect. No further details are given for this complex organization, but a somewhat cryptic requirement stated is that all signatories must 'be treated equally.'

While the new division is under construction, its affairs are in the hands of a coordinating council consisting of two representatives of each signatory and one each from banks providing credit, the *komora* and the city government. The council is to be dissolved when the division is formally established, and then 'a new joint body of similar nature' will be formed 'to coordinate development and business policy' (article 15). The extent of the authority of this body is not specified, but it is likely to be some sort of joint business council similar to those set up by BIGZ–MATROZ and IMT–IMR (the next case). Like those, this council would serve as a mechanism for allowing adaptive, sequential decision-making.

The very first article of this agreement makes clear the reasons for undertaking this project. With very little rhetoric about the importance of meeting society's needs, it states that the signatories want to increase their productive capacity and hence their incomes. Article 2 explicitly states as goals of the agreement not only the greater availability of concrete, but also the signatories' share in the income created by the proposed new division.

This agreement is more specific about income distribution than is the broad agreement that covers all of the divisions. It states that income will be shared in proportion to contributions of total, current and past labor.[2] As in the previous case, this amounts to a sharing clause that allows the use of incomplete long-term contracts. But first there must be set aside, from joint income, funds sufficient to pay to the division's workers personal income and collective consumption in amounts equal to the average received by workers in the enterprises that sign the agreement.

There is a rather complicated section (article 8) that deals with repayment of credit supplied by banks. At the time Vacić's book was written, this matter had not been settled. The tentative wording specifies that out of the revenue earned by the division there must be set aside (before joint income is calculated) money to repay the credit arranged by the signatories. Under this arrangement the money destined for credit repayment is technically income of the division and the division is therefore responsible for the 'legal obligations' on those funds (social security contributions, *komora* fees, national defense tax, insurance, etc.). Alternative versions of article 8 offer two other proposals. One is that amortization funds be used for all or part of the credit payments. This is not usually allowed and hence would require special government approval. The other is that the signatories pay off the bank credit out of their shares of the joint income, which will be larger if credit payments are not subtracted from the division's revenue. The signatories would then bear responsibility for paying the 'legal obligations' on that part of the income. The division itself would prefer either of these two alternatives over the tentative wording.

What remains, after subtracting from the division's revenue personal income and collective consumption for the division's workers and funds for repayment of credit, is 'joint income'. This is to be divided between the division and the signatories of the agreement. The division gets a share based on its contribution of current labor, valued at the average earnings of labor during the first year of operation, i.e. at the average earnings of labor among the signatories during that year. The share of the signatories is based on their contribution of funds (exclusive of the credit they arranged). That is, the division's share of joint income is equal to the value of labor divided by the sum of the value of labor plus the funds supplied by the signatories. The share of each signatory in joint income is equal to his contribution divided by the sum of labor value plus the total of funds contributed by all signatories.

These shares are determined by the proportions calculated for the first year and remain fixed as long as the right to a share of income remains. Subsequent variations in labor input will not affect these shares. This puts the founders in the position of wanting to maximize total profit, whereas the workers in the division want to maximize profit per worker. Thus, control over labor input is of some importance. The extent of the founders' influence in this respect is not clear from this agreement, but certainly in principle the workers in the cement division should have the decisive role.

The founders' right to a share of income lasts until their own funds (not bank credit) have been repaid. The return to the signatories of their invested funds comes out of the division's share of joint income and does not begin until after bank credit is fully paid off. Article 11 calls for repayment of the signatories' investments in not less than ten and not more than twenty-five years after the bank loans are repaid. The details of these payments are to be negotiated between the division and the signatories after the division is formally established.

IMT and IMR

The fourth case is an agreement between Industrija Mašina i Traktora (IMT), a maker of agricultural tractors in New Belgrade, and Industrija Motora iz Rakovice (IMR), a manufacturer of engines in nearby

Rakovica. The essence of the agreement is that IMR will supply IMT with engines for its tractors. More precisely, the agreement is signed by the tractor division of IMT and by the diesel motor division of IMR.

The agreement specifies numbers of tractors and engines of each model and horsepower for each year, as well as dinars worth of spare parts. While the duration of the agreement is for 'an indefinite time', the numbers are given for each of the first five years and for the tenth year. Both sides retain the right to cancel at any time with at least three (or six[3]) months' notice, but whichever side cancels is obliged to continue to deliver any parts needed by the other or to take delivery of any output from the other side until the other can make alternative arrangements (but not for more than three years).

At the time this agreement was drawn up, IMT and IMR had been doing business with each other for many years. In fact, at an earlier time they had both been members of a large, loose-knit conglomerate (Udružena Metalska Industrija), which subsequently fell apart. They had a history of disagreements about the prices and delivery schedules of motors, about the sale of spare parts and about the distribution of foreign exchange earnings. This agreement is intended to settle these conflicts.

In principle, the agreement is also supposed to specify the relationship among all of the firms that supply parts for these tractors. That would include a foundry, a ball bearing maker, a machine tool firm and others, in addition to IMT and IMR. The agreement specifies that it is 'open' and that 'any basic organization of associated labor whose production is in the long-run tied to this joint product' can join the agreement 'under the same terms' as the signatories (articles 2 and 3). However, in fact no specifics for other firms are included.

The agreement is clearly more than a simple contract to deliver a fixed number of diesel engines. It includes joint development of additional production capacity and requires (article 10) exclusive dealing on both sides for output produced with the new capacity: IMT will use only engines from IMR, and IMR will sell engines to no other tractor maker. Furthermore, work connected with this agreement is to take priority over any other work either firm undertakes. If any wholesale or retail trade organizations join the agreement, they are prohibited from selling any other tractors, domestic or foreign, as long as IMT is able to supply all their needs. In addition to jointly approaching banks for funding, the partners may lend directly to one another. Whenever possible the two will deal with purchasing and inventories jointly. Sales policy, including the price of the final product, will be decided jointly, and foreign exchange earnings will be divided proportionately. As in the previous two cases, the agreement provides for creation of a joint council to make major decisions. In this case there are to be three delegates from each side. The delegates may be workers from the divisions that are the signatories to the agreement or they may be from other divisions of the enterprises to which they belong. If a council decision is not unanimous, the matter is to be referred to the partners' own decision-making bodies. As a final resort, disputes can be referred to a court at the republican *komora*.

It is difficult to classify this agreement in terms of the distinction discussed in chapters 1 and 4 between two different approaches to joint activity: (1) market coordination governed by a contract between autonomous buyer and seller, and (2) joint decision-making by what is essentially a single economic unit. To some extent both apply, but what we have here is essentially a limited merger. Although a considerable portion of the agreement is devoted to sorting out exactly which costs and which revenues are and are not subject to sharing, it is interesting that the terms 'internal trade' and 'internal prices' are used in the agreement (articles 54 and 55) to refer to transactions between IMT and IMR. That is, they refer to these transactions as though they were within an enterprise. Further, although the agreement does specify a procedure for calculating transfer prices, they are to be used only for a temporary distribution of earnings. Subsequent readjustments substantially reduce their importance and the final distribution of income is determined by calculating each side's contribution to total output. Perhaps the strongest evidence that there is a *de facto* merger here is the fact that many decisions that might be left to the downstream partner are to be decided by a joint council, which is the vehicle for implementing a system that incorporates both the adaptive, sequential decision-making and the sharing clause described in chapter 4.

The key to understanding the nature of the relationship between IMT and IMR is found in articles 54 and 55 of their self-management agreement. The former specifies that 'income generated under this agreement is to be distributed according to component parts of the joint product, which, together with the costs of business, determine internal prices'. This sounds like a buyer–seller relationship, and would be if the internal prices were set and held constant (at least until some agreed-upon renegotiation date). Even the fact that a change in the price of input materials of more than 3 per cent requires recalculation of internal prices is not unusual in a market contract between buyer and seller. However, article 54 goes on to specify that 'a change in the selling price of the final product, in any amount, causes a change in the internal price . . .'. This makes the internal prices seem more like a device for sharing income within a single economic unit than a mechanism for coordinating autonomous entities. This view is supported by article 55, which states that, during the year, payments between IMT and IMR are made using 'temporary' internal prices that change with changes in the prices of materials from outside and with the price of the final product.

Fully to understand the process of income distribution, we must realize that there are two mechanisms operating simultaneously: (1) during the year, transfer prices based on costs are used to determine payments between the parties; (2) at the end of the year, total net income is divided up between the participants on the basis of their proportional contributions to total production. If the distribution that resulted from the transfer prices is not the same as that implied by the end-of-year calculation of proportional contributions, then, in order to conform to the latter, 'contribtutions of income are made to that partner to whom ... the difference belongs' (article 55).

Let us look first at what underlies the transfer prices. The agreement is based on what Vacić calls the 'cost principle', i.e. transfer prices are supposed to equal the sum of raw material, capital and labor costs for each intermediate product. Overhead costs are included by calculating the proportion of each division's total output that is involved in the joint project and multiplying that by its total overhead. Capital is measured by amortization payments that are specified by law. Labor is measured using norms that are set out in great detail in an appendix to the agreement. For every intermediate good, production time is measured in units of a standard unskilled worker. The criteria are based on 'the technologically determined production time of each part, ... and the operational complexity of the work' (article 50). Articles 28 and 29 specify that productivity norms are initially based on 1976 performance and must increase yearly. Article 53 states that norms are to be specified at the end of each year for the following year. Vacić recommends (1976, p. 367) that they be set less often, once every three years, with each division being required to increase productivity by an agreed percentage each year. If they exceed that commitment they should, according to Vacić, keep for themselves the difference in earnings.

'The monetary value of current labor comes from grouping similar categories of work in terms of the standard unskilled worker and multiplying by the minimum wage of the enterprise to which the division belongs' (article 51). Vacić argues (1976, p. 350) that they should use the previous year's average wage for each division, but the agreement specifies instead that they use the guaranteed minimum stated in each firm's rulebook.

Now consider the second mechanism – proportional contributions to total production. Article 54 states that 'the basis for distribution of income by component parts is the current and past labor embodied in each part'. 'Past labor' is a euphemism for capital that the Yugoslavs use to justify paying a return to a firm or division that supplies funds for a project. So this mechanism, like the transfer price mechanism, requires a detailed calculation of each firm's labor and capital inputs.

At the time Vacić wrote his book, the agreement between IMT and IMR had not yet been signed and some disputes had not yet been settled. These disagreements are in themselves quite interesting because they illustrate the partners' different attitudes towards certain matters, including the extent to which each retains some independence.

The major dispute is embodied in article 9, which appears in Vacić's book in two versions. As proposed by IMT, the article specifies that in calculating the total value of joint production each tractor is valued as though sold with a minimum set of equipment. The IMR version of article 9, however, includes in the total value of joint production all equipment that is 'functionally related to the joint product . . . or that appears on the same invoice'. Clearly, IMR was trying to lay claim to a share of the earnings on products that it does not itself produce, e.g. hydraulic lifts, which are optional equipment.

The other major point of contention concerns input prices. The joint earnings that will be divided between the partners are defined as revenue from the sale of the joint product minus costs of production. Included in those costs are the costs of materials used. IMT's version of article 46, which defines those costs, specifies that the calculations will use planned costs, while IMR's version specifies actual costs. The difference is that under IMT's version any unexpected variation in input prices is borne by (or benefits) only the division that purchases those inputs. Under IMR's version, the burden or benefit is shared by both.

This procedure for adjusting transfer prices raises the fundamental question of the supplier's incentive to minimize costs. To the extent that it can pass on increased material costs, its incentive to find less expensive inputs is diminished, although not totally eliminated since it knows that the demand for its product is a derived demand that depends on the price of the final product. A higher transfer price means a higher price for the final product and hence a lower quantity demanded of the parts it produces. Clearly, IMT's wording of article 54 (that deviations of actual performance from anticipated norms redound to the benefit or harm of the responsible partner) is intended to insure appropriate incentives.

The notion that they should remain at least to a limited extent independent units each working for its own profit is also evident in a dispute over article 54: in wording proposed by IMT and opposed by IMR, article 54 specifies that 'business results of each partner . . . resulting from deviation of actual quantities from the agreed upon norms . . . fall to each partner's own benefit or harm'.

Another problem area was the extent to which spare parts production is included in the joint project. Articles 35 to 37 of the agreement settle the matter by stating that the parties will jointly create a network of spare parts warehouses and sales offices. Each will carefully document the extent to which its costs and revenues connected with spare parts production are attributable to the joint products (as opposed to spare parts related to other production outside this agreement). It is explicitly stated that revenue from spare parts sales not transacted through the joint distribution network is not to be shared.

Petar Drapsin, Dvadeset Prvi Mai and Crvena Zastava

This case study is of an agreement involving three firms: Petar Drapsin (PD), located in Mladenovac, makes light alloy metal castings; Dvadeset Prvi Mai (DPM), in Belgrade, makes internal combustion engines; and Crvena Zastava (CZ), located in Kragujevac, makes the Yugoslav version of Fiat automobiles. Kragujevac is about 100 kilometers south of Belgrade and Mladenovac is about half way between Kragujevac and Belgrade. Over many years these firms have done a considerable amount of business together: PD supplied castings to both DPM and CZ, and DPM supplied engines to CZ.

Reflecting a shortage of domestically produced light metal castings, PD was not able to produce enough output to meet the needs of the other firms. Primarily for this reason, they agreed to contribute funds towards expansion of the production capacity at PD. The agreement specifies amounts and types of castings to be produced and delivered to DPM and CZ. In addition to the greater availability of a needed input, another inducement to contribute funds is the expectation of a share in the income of PD. The goals explicitly stated in the first two articles of the agreement include production of output 'for their own needs and for the market', 'coordination of development' and 'increasing their income by participating in jointly created income'.

The agreement calls for building a factory with output capacity of 7,068 tons annually of light metal alloy castings. The factory will operate as part of the already existing castings division of PD. The project will require 86.7 million dinars (approximately $4.8 million) for fixed capital and 35 million dinars (approximately $1.9 million) for working capital. DPM and CZ are to put in 8 million dinars and 6 million dinars, respectively, which will be used for fixed capital. The castings division of PD will provide (from its own funds or credit it arranges) the remaining 72.7 million dinars for fixed capital and all of the working capital.

An explicit part of the agreement (article 9) is that DPM and CZ get priority over other buyers in the delivery of castings. If output is not enough to meet their needs, they will get deliveries in proportion to their investments. Interestingly, this right to priority treatment does not end with the return of the invested funds. Article 10 states that it continues as long as PD is in the business of making castings.

The calculations prescribed in this agreement are somewhat harder to follow than those in the other cases. This is because, in principle, PD is sharing in the income of DPM and CZ as well as vice versa. That is, in this case there is an effort simultaneously to let PD share in the final price (and variation thereof) of engines and automobiles and to let DPM and CZ earn a return on their investment in DP's expanded production capacity. Furthermore, unlike the cases of BIGZ–MATROZ and Mali Makiš, where transfer prices are supposed to be an average of market prices, this case is like that of IMT–IMR, where the internal price is intended to achieve a particular income distribution: 'Division of joint income realized from the sale of engines and other products using castings is achieved via the prices of castings in mutual trade' (article 12).

The sharing of income realized from the sale of final products is achieved by calculating the internal price of castings as follows: first, an income 'index' is found by dividing the net income realized from the sale of engines and other final products by the value of the sum of all past labor (i.e. capital) and current labor expended by all participants in producing these goods (article 14). This index is then multiplied by the value of labor (both past and current) necessary to produce a casting; the product of that multiplication is the income that PD should earn on that casting. This income is added to the cost of the casting to determine the price of the casting.

This method clearly reflects its designers' training in Marxist labor theory of value. In order to avoid circularity (net income cannot both depend on labor value and be used to determine labor value), a standard value of labor must be assumed. How this is to be calculated is not clear from the agreement, but Vacić proposes an elaborate system that uses national average output per worker to calculate a value for a standard unskilled worker. An agreed set of norms specifies labor input in terms of standard unskilled workers for each casting and each final product. Then the monetary value of current labor can be found by multiplying income per standard worker by the number of standard workers. The value of past labor is found by taking the average value of fixed and working capital used.

Other definitions are necessary, too. The agreement states that the non-labor cost of a product consists of material costs plus amortization of the capital used in production. Material cost is determined by a set of jointly agreed-upon norms for materials, energy and small tools.

Amortization is based on the purchase price, the official depreciation index and what the agreement calls 'rational use of installed capacity' (article 13). Indirect costs are also included before income is added to get the price of the casting. Net income from final sales is gross revenue minus both labor and non-labor costs.

We should notice that use of this index is mathematically equivalent to taking PD's labor as a percentage of total labor and multiplying by net income:

$$\frac{NI}{TL} \times PD_L = \frac{PD_L}{TL} \times NI$$

where NI is net income from final sales
TL is the value of the sum of all labor used, and
PD_L is the value of PD's labor.

The first term on the left is the index used in the agreement. Clearly, the result is that PD gets a share of net income that is equal to its share of total (past and current) labor.

The second part of the two-way income sharing is DPM's and CZ's share of DP's income. Article 18 specifies that income from the expanded casting production is to be divided among the three participants 'in proportion to funds invested'. As in the BIGZ–MATROZ and Mali Makiš cases, the income that is to be shared among the investors is calculated only after subtracting from revenue enough funds to provide workers in the casting division with personal incomes and collective consumption comparable[4] to those of workers in the other investing firms. Each investor's share counts as part of its total business income for that year and hence each will pay the usual 'legal obligations' (social security, etc.) on that income (article 21).

As required by the Constitution, the agreement specifies termination of the part of the sharing arrangement that is based on invested funds when the full value of those funds is returned. It is made explicit (article 19) that the investors have a right to the return of their invested funds *in addition* to a share of income. Although article 18 refers to return of the 'full value' of the invested funds, article 19 explicitly states that it is the 'nominal sum' that is to be returned. That is, there is no provision for compensation for inflation. It is the castings division, not the PD enterprise, that is legally required to repay the investment. It is given the option of doing so out of its own share of the joint income, out of amortization funds or from other assets. Repayment is to be accomplished in eight equal annual installments beginning the first full business year after the start of regular production.

Sharing of income in the other direction, i.e. PD's share of the income realized from the sale of final products, need not have a termination specified. This is because it is based on pooling labor from both sides.

The agreement also specifies the possibility of termination in case any of the parties fails to meet its obligations. If the agreement is broken through the fault of the castings division, it will be required to repay any remaining unpaid debt in a period 'twice as short' as the eight equal payments otherwise called for. If the others are at fault, the division has up to twice that eight-year period to repay.

Statements about the extent of each participant's legal liabilities are a bit confusing. On the one hand, article 22 says that for debts that result from the agreement 'each participant is responsible up to the amount of funds which he invested'. This sounds like a traditional limited liability contract. On the other hand, article 7 states that, if the cost of the project exceeds expectations, they will contribute the necessary additional funds in proportion to the initially invested amounts. Furthermore, article 25 requires that if the division runs a loss after construction is completed, each participant must contribute to correction of the problem (*sanitacija*) in proportion to those initial amounts.

The agreement provides that a participant may transfer his rights and obligations in the venture to an outside party only with the approval of the other participants. It is interesting that the notion of transferability, however limited, appears at all.

Like the previous cases studied, this agreement calls for creation of a joint business council that makes possible adaptive, sequential decision-making whenever needed on matters not settled by the initial incomplete contract. Two delegates are to be named by each of the three partners, and the six will then choose a president from among themselves. Decisions require a majority vote.

KLEK

Further support for the general principles that emerge from these first five cases can be found in studies by other scholars. Ellen Comisso (1979, 1980) and Kenneth Zapp (1983) studied several Yugoslav firms in considerable detail. The wide diversity that Comisso reports (1980, p. 202) is also evident in Zapp's study of eight firms, despite the further implementation of the system of autonomous divisions between 1974, when Comisso did her field research, and 1979–80, when Zapp did his. But the evidence of both is broadly consistent with the picture presented in this book. In particular, Zapp confirms my views on the extent of competition in Yugoslav industry and on capital flows. Both he and Comisso find evidence of extensive and meaningful autonomy of divisions within firms, including a system of transfer prices that in many cases reflects prices on outside markets. Income distribution and decision-making mechanisms in all cases can be viewed, to use Williamson's terminology, as sharing clauses and procedures for adaptive, sequential decision-making.

Comisso tells us (1980, p. 202) that, initially, decentralization at some enterprises was only formal, and in fact decision-making power remained at the center. However, she also says that passage of the new Constitution 'weakened enterprise hierarchies'. At KLEK (a name she made up to hide the identity of the enterprise she studied in detail), the divisionalized structure 'permitted some units to escape the control of the others, . . . a process . . . which had already been under way for some time' (1979, p. 232). The extent of divisional autonomy varies even within the firm and seems to depend in part on personalities: division II at KLEK 'tended to resolve most of it own problems independently and rarely required approval from either the central self-management bodies or other division councils' (1979, p. 230). Division III, on the other hand, was rather inactive and avoided exercising its decision-making power until new elections put a more dynamic person in as head; it then became quite independent. Division I made its own decisions but frequently sent reports to and deferred to the central workers' council. The shift of power from the center to the divisions was reflected in the declining frequency of central workers' council meetings, and would have been carried even further if KLEK had completed the transfer of funds to the divisions. Yet despite the real autonomy of its divisions, there are circumstances under which KLEK displays sufficient solidarity and unity to justify regarding it as a single enterprise (Comisso, 1979, pp. 188–98).

The Zapp Cases

On the question of competition vs. collusion in the Yugoslav economy, Zapp's case studies are illustrative of the point of view I take in chapters 1 and 2. 'Aggressive competition' and 'intense competition' are terms he uses (pp. 201 and 203) to describe the cardboard box industry. He found that self-management agreements, both within and between firms, are not always effective: in one publishing firm, 'some 40 other self-management agreements were signed to satisfy legal requirements but seem to have little or no influence on BOAL income earning and distribution' (p. 157). 'The Composite Organization of which Tvornica Duhan Zagreb [Tobacco Factory of Zagreb] is one member operates only on paper. Its members do not have agreements on income distribution, investments, associated means, working capital, or production capacity' (p. 163). He tells us (p. 165) that planned capacity expansion in the tobacco industry exceeds total expected demand. On the other hand, there are two industries where Zapp does find some price fixing and market sharing – soft drinks and electronics. But in both of these cases the collusion is limited to Croatian firms. He points out that competition with Slovenian electronics producers remains unsuppressed.

All of Zapp's cases support the view that divisions have considerable autonomy. For example, at Mladinska Knjiga (a book publisher) 'Virtually all income is earned and capital allocated independently by the various BOALs. The ability of each to compete on the market seems to be the principle determinant of income earning. Neither income nor risk are shared by the BOALs' (1983, pp. 156–7). The printing division must compete with outside firms for printing jobs and about one-third of the firm's books are printed by other companies. Furthermore, the printing division gets only about half its work from within the corporation.

At Ivica Lovinčić, a maker of cardboard boxes, divisions are free to buy spare parts for their machines either from their own parts division or from outside. Apparently, only infrequent exercise of the right to buy outside is sufficient to keep the internal price down.

Zapp shows that at both INA (a petroleum firm) and Litostroj (a maker of heavy industrial equipment) some internal prices are set to equal market prices: the Sisak refinery buys crude from other parts of INA at the world price and the education division of Litostroj charges sister divisions the same fees for worker training as it charges outside firms. However, at Mladinska Knjiga the firm's own retail stores buy books at prices 25 per cent below the prices charged to unrelated retailers.

Internal prices for services provided by work communities, such as repairs, cleaning and bookkeeping, are paid for by each user division and are priced per hour, per square foot, etc. At Litostroj, rates per hour for technical drawing and machine testing are negotiated every six months. At Ivica Lovinčić, negotiations to set the hourly rate for special parts fabrication by the spare parts division are annual. Certainly these arrangements fit the ideas of chapter 3, where it was shown that the internal sale of services can result in efficiently reallocating labor. However, at both firms, year-end adjustments are made so that personal incomes in work communities reflect the extent to which the enterprise fulfilled its annual plan.

On the matter of income distribution, both Comisso and Zapp agree that (1) in principle each worker's income depends primarily on the performance of his own division, and (2) in fact, in some cases workers' incomes depend in part on the performance of the other divisions in the firm. Thus, actual income differentials are sometimes smaller than true earnings differentials, and some divisions in effect subsidize others. For example, at Križevci Trgovačno, a food processor, income differentials between workers with similar jobs 'arise from differences in each BOAL's degree of plan achievement' (Zapp, 1983, p. 169). Similarly, at Litostroj 'personal income is derived by multiplying each worker's point total [a measure of technical skill, responsibility, unpleasantness of the work, etc.] times his or her BOAL's income per point which depends on its overall business success' (Zapp, 1983, p. 192). However, the central workers' council at Litostroj voted to set a 5 per cent maximum on the amount by which income per point at any division could exceed the average across all divisions. At Nikola Tesla, the maximum amount by which average income in any division is allowed to exceed the income average across all other divisions is 10 per cent. This limit is in fact a binding constraint on the installation division, where incomes would otherwise be higher. The installers, like division II at KLEK, are subsidizing their sister divisions.

In many firms the distribution of income among divisions depends in part on a system of standard costs. For example, at LEK, a pharmaceutical company, the chemical division provides inputs to the cosmetics division. Then the income from final sale of the finished products is divided between them in proportions determined by a system of annually negotiated standard costs. A similar system of standard costs is used to divide enterprise income among the producer divisions at Litostroj, where the proportions are renegotiated twice a year. At LEK, the work communities get a fixed percentage, set annually, of the enterprise's gross income.

Zapp provides a number of examples of interfirm capital flows motivated by the desire of the investor to improve the supply of some important input. For example, Mladinska Knjiga loaned 10 million dinars to a firm that supplies paper to its printing division. The money was to be repaid in ten years without interest. Apparently, the prospect of improved availability of paper was sufficient inducement to giant the loan. On the other hand, a loan from Ivica Lovinčić, also to a paper supplier, requires interest payments as well as guaranteed supply of specific quantities of paper. Capital flows within the firm at Litostroj had carried a small fee (2–5 per cent) until 1980 when the interest charge was dropped: enterprise solidarity and/or the prospect of a sister division's growth was sufficient motivation. In another case, LEK invested in another enterprise's chemical processing plant in return for a share in its income and increased access to its product.

Summary

A major point of this chapter is that lending between economic units other than banks results in the realization of projects that otherwise probably would not have been undertaken. In the cellulose and aluminium castings cases, the workers in the enterprise where the new factory would be located were unable or unwilling to provide all of the necessary money from their own pockets or from retained earnings. In the case of concrete, there was no parent enterprise to provide funds. Financial arrangements for expanded production in the tractor deal are not clear from the agreement, but lending between the partners is mentioned. The textile firm's document does not specify a major project but it does include arrangements for interdivisional capital flows. In some cases, banks provided some of the money, but Yugoslav banks will not provide 100 per cent financing for new investment.

There appear to be two major motivating factors behind these joint investment projects: increasing the availability of some needed input, and a simple profit motive. BIGZ sought increased supplies of newsprint for its publications, the founders of Mali Makiš sought more concrete for their construction work, IMT wanted a reliable supply of diesel engines, and Crvena Zastava and Dvadeset Prvi Mai wanted more aluminum castings. Zapp's description of Mladinska Knjiga, Ivica Lovinčić and LEK provides further examples. Virtually all of the agreements make quite explicit the participants' search for more profits. That they are willing to tie up money for as much as fifteen years indicates that those who supplied funds do not anticipate finding better uses for that money within their own divisions during that time period. Those who will have to repay the loans apparently are willing to take on that burden eventually; or else their time horizons are such that they see the burden as falling on their successors. It is impossible to know whether the decisions to undertake these projects were dependent upon the inflation argument presented in chapter 5, but, given the high inflation rate (10–25 per cent in those years), workers would certainly be attracted to opportunities to invest in real assets.

In nearly all of the cases studied in this chapter the major problem of joint activity seems to be the measurement of each party's contribution to production and hence its share of income. In the first three cases (Varteks, BIGZ–MATROZ, Mali Makiš), transfer prices are based on outside prices and income distribution is in turn largely determined by transfer prices. Certainly in these cases resource allocation is affected by transfer prices because divisions base production decisions on them. In the next two cases (IMT–IMR and PD–DPR–CZ), income distribution is based on calculations of labor and other inputs, and transfer prices are then adjusted so as to effect that distribution of income. Similarly, in Zapp's description of LEK there appears the use of standard costs to distribute income among divisions. And even in those of Zapp's cases (INA and Litostroj) where some transfer prices are determined by outside market prices, income distribution involves some adjustments that complicate the relationship between prices and incomes. But it is possible to argue (as I did in chapters 1, 3 and 4) that even in those cases where transfer prices are determined *after* production decisions are made, those decisions are based on expectations derived from previous years' transfer prices. Thus, resource allocation is affected by transfer prices but with a lag.

One of the most interesting characteristics of some of these arrangements is the fact that some workers are not entirely residual claimants. In the paper, cement and castings cases, workers in the division in which the new investment takes place are guaranteed personal incomes and collective consumption on a par with the workers in the contributing divisions. This is not to say there is no variability in their incomes, but only that the variability is not exclusively tied to their own division's performance. Fluctuations in the profitability of their own division is diluted by the participation of other workers, and indirectly their own income depends on the success of those other divisions. At the same time, workers in the divisions that are providing investment funds are sharing the risks of the project because the return on their investment depends on the success of the project.

Something that is quite obvious, but so important as to warrant stating explicitly, is the fact that, in the Yugoslav system, capital (which they call past labor) is a legitimate basis for income distribution. Firms that have control over substantial sums, of either their own money or borrowed funds, can and do use that money to earn money. But as long as these sums of money are controlled by groups of workers, rather than by individuals, one could argue that there is no serious conflict with the ideology of socialism.

In several of these cases it is difficult to tell whether we are dealing with one enterprise or two. But whether it appears to be a single firm with autonomous divisions or separate firms with closely engaged divisions, certain characteristics are present: a joint business council makes decisions over time as cirumstances require, and an income-sharing arrangement exists so that each unit has an interest in the success of the overall project. These are exactly the ideas that in chapter 4 were seen to be the essential characteristics of the Yugoslav firm: adaptive, sequential decision-making combined with a sharing clause allows independent divisions to rely on incomplete long-term contracts.

Notes

1 *Komora* is usually translated as Economic Chamber or Chamber of Commerce, which is the American/English institution that most nearly corresponds to the Yugoslav *komora*. However, the Yugoslav *komora* does more than represent the interests of its members; it plays a very active role in influencing and coordinating their activities.
2 Since total labor equals current labor plus past labor, this formulation is redundant.
3 At the time Vacić's book was written, there was a dispute over how much notice should be required.
4 Translated literally, the wording specifies that the income and collective consumption of the casting division workers will be 'in accordance with the joint bases and measurements [criteria] for distribution of these funds which are in effect in the organizations of associated labor of the participants'.

7 Divisionalization in Other Socialist Countries

Introduction

The purpose of this chapter is to show that the concepts of divisionalization developed in previous chapters are not unique to Yugoslavia. On the the contrary, similar matters have been the focus of attention in the Soviet Union and the socialist countries of Eastern Europe for much of the past two decades. While most of these countries have not yet made any fundamental changes in their planning systems, they have experimented with changes in the size of basic economic units and with their administrative organizational structure. Many of the ideas developed in previous chapters in connection with large Yugoslav firms have implications that are relevant to the efficiency of the associations, trusts, *kombinats*, etc., that are increasingly important in the Soviet Union and Eastern Europe.

Concern with the optimal size of enterprises and with the mechanism coordinating them represents a major shift from an earlier attitude. Lenin said that under socialism the basic organizational task was 'the transformation of the whole of the state economic mechanism into a single huge machine'. When the task is completed, he said, 'the whole of society will have become one office and one factory'. Most of the socialist countries took this to mean that all that was needed was a mechanism for communicating commands. The enterprise itself would be no more than a small cog in a well-oiled machine and could be assumed to operate correctly. Enterprises, it seemed, could be put in the hands of clerks like those who run post offices.[1]

For decades the Soviets adjusted and modified their economic system, continually changing managers' quotas and bonus rates, in an effort to ensure that they did what the planners wanted them to do. Then, after more than thirty years of central planning, they began to see that they needed a better mechanism for coordinating decisions rather than just a hierarchy for disaggregating commands and enforcing compliance.

The associations that have developed in the Soviet-type economies bear substantial similarities to Yugoslav enterprise structure. The fundamental similarity is the notion of groups of subunits that relate to one another more directly than do subunits that are not grouped together. It is possible to draw the analogy between socialist associations and Yugoslav enterprises at two different levels. In terms of size, and because both consist of a number of smaller units, it is natural to think of the association as corresponding to a Yugoslav enterprise; but it is sometimes instructive to think of the association itself as a division of a larger unit. That is, we can think of an entire industry as a giant enterprise that is divisionalized into a number of more or less autonomous associations. Thus the associations can be thought of as corresponding either to the divisions of the Yugoslav enterprise or to the enterprise itself. There is no reason why the analysis cannot be applied at both levels.

Of course, there are important differences between Yugoslavia and the other socialist countries. Most evident are the limited authority of the subunits in the other socialist countries to make important decisions and the absence of a market relationship among them. In Yugoslavia, the relationships outside the enterprise are market relationships, while in the Soviet Union and Eastern Europe the economic mechanism outside the association is central planning. But in both cases the reason for creating the enterprise or association is to avoid some of the costs of using the outside mechanism. By grouping enterprises into associations, the Soviet and Eastern European countries are facilitating direct communication and closer relationships between supplier and user or among users without interposing the central planners. The associations are a means of avoiding planners' inefficiencies just as Yugoslav enterprises, by reducing opportunism, make market transactions less costly.

With the exception of Hungary, there has so far been no substantial movement towards a market system among the Soviet-type economies. But the creation of these associations can be seen as a first step toward creating the industrial organization and corporate relationships that would be useful if and when those countries do so. Both the associations and the subunits within them do more than accept instructions from above. The subunits especially engage in some mutual negotiations that result in contracts, agreements, trades, etc. Of course, the major obstacle to the adoption of a market system is the absence of true scarcity prices. They are the rocks on which most attempted reforms have foundered.

I do not mean to suggest that the associations are consciously intended as preparation for the introduction of a market system or that they will be useful only in that context. Every economic system consists of a set of organizations. If there are costs associated with transactions between them, then it matters how they are grouped. The socialist associations represent first tentative steps in the direction of the multidivisional corporate structure that was adopted first in the capitalist countries and later in Yugoslavia. That structure has advantages in a planned as well as in a market system.

In the first part of this chapter I review the changes in industrial structure that have taken place in the Soviet Union and Eastern Europe and some of the conventional explanations for these changes. Then I examine their significance from the point of view of transaction costs.

Changes in the Organizational Structure of Socialist Industry

An important characteristic common to the many reforms that took place during the 1960s and 1970s, in Eastern Europe as well as in the Soviet Union, was the creation of industrial associations. Also called firms, trusts, combines, unions and big enterprises, these organizations were formed by the merger of several enterprises. They began to appear in 1958, first in Poland and then in Czechoslovakia and the German Democratic Republic. In 1961 the Soviet Union followed suit. Numerous mergers took place in Hungary and Bulgaria in 1963, and Romania finally followed along in 1969. In most countries the mergers, or a second wave of consolidation, were effected just before or during major economic reforms.

Among the East European countries the number and size of enterprises merged to form associations vary considerably. In Czechoslovakia, 1,417 enterprises were merged in to 253 units in 1958 and subsequently further consolidated into 102 'production-economic units', thus averaging about fourteen enterprises per association.[2] In Romania, the number of enterprises per association ranges from four to sixty-two, with the average number of employees being 30,000. In Poland, the number of plants per enterprise increased from 7.9 in 1965 to 11.8 in 1975. The number of Polish workers per association varies from 9,000 to 70,000. As a result of the creation of the associations, the total number of separate enterprises in Hungary fell from 1,368 in 1960 to 702 in 1979, while the proportion of firms with more than 1,000 workers increased from 15 per cent to 45 per cent. In East Germany, the number of firms fell by more than 50 per cent. In Bulgaria, nearly all industrial enterprises were grouped into 120 associations in 1963 and then further consolidated into sixty-five associations in 1971.

Creation of associations was particularly important in the Soviet Union because of its large number of very small enterprises. In 1968, one-third of all Soviet industrial enterprises employed fewer than 100 workers and accounted for less than 5 per cent of total output; 56 per cent (over 28,000 enterprises) had fewer than 200 workers and accounted for only 12 per cent of gross output. In manufacturing alone there were 18,079 enterprises with fewer than 500 workers.[3] By comparison, divisions of Yugoslav enterprises typically have between 100 and 500 workers.

The creation of associations began in the Soviet Union with the merger of five shoe plants in Lvov in 1961.[4] In that particular case the initiative came from the plant managers themselves and from local Party leaders, but the idea was picked up at the national level and an ambitious program of mergers was announced as part of Kosygin's 1965 reform program. By the beginning of 1973 there were 1,101 industrial associations encompassing approximately 4,500 enterprises, or 9 per cent of all industrial enterprises. Then in April 1973 all industrial ministries were told to prepare immediately plans to merge all enterprises into several types of associations. The simplest type is called a production association and typically includes four or five production enterprises that produce similar or related products. It has been suggested that the typical size of production associations will be increased to seven enterprises. In some cases an association includes all of the enterprises in a particular industry, in which case it is called an industrial association and includes production associations as some of its members. If a research institute is included, then it is called a science–production association. Associations may be organized along geographical lines and/or product lines and may be based on a vertical relationship as well.

In 1973 it was announced that all industrial enterprises would be merged into associations by 1975, but that goal was delayed until 1980 and still has not been realized. By the end of 1977 there were 3,670 associations encompassing 16,515 enterprises, or about one-third of the 50,000 industrial enterprises in the Soviet Union. The size of Soviet production associations varies from under 500 workers to over 100,000 workers, but over half of them employ 1,000–5,000 workers, which is comparable to a medium-size Yugoslav enterprise.

Associations are also being formed in the trade and construction sectors and to combine agro-industrial activities.

Conventional Explanations for the Changes in Organizational Structure

A number of benefits were expected to result from these mergers. First, the change can be seen as an effort to reduce the amount of information (i.e. the degree of detail) flowing from the center and to shorten the lines of command to the enterprises. Reduction in the number of basic units that the central planners have to deal with should reduce the amount of calculation they have to do and thus lessen the overall planning burden at the center. Of course, there would be a corresponding increase in planning work to be done at the level of the association, but the hope was that executives on the spot would be able to handle the additional work and the combined effect would be a net decrease in administrative personnel. Thus the reorganization was largely an effort to reverse, or at least to slow, the rapid rate of growth of administrative personnel, which in the Soviet Union had been nearly twice the rate of growth of overall employment. Between 1966 and 1977 the size of the Soviet bureaucracy had increased by 57 per cent while total state employment had increased by only 38 per cent (Hohmann *et al.*, 1975, p. 10; Schroeder, 1979, p. 314).

In Eastern Europe, too, the associations were expected to achieve substantial economies of scale in management. Woroniak (1969, p. 270) claims that one of the objectives in the creation of associations was conservation of scarce managerial skills. Similarly, in talking about the Polish reform, Zielinski (1973, pp. 247–8 and 281) points to the need to achieve economies of scale by concentrating highly qualified personnel, and Keren (1973, pp. 136–7) tells us that reducing the center's cost of allocating funds by reducing the number of peripheral units with which it had to deal was a major factor in the East German reform. However, evidence on the actual effect on the number of administrative personnel is conflicting: Gorlin (1976b, p. 66n) reports several instances where administrative expenses were reduced by the creation of associations in the Soviet Union, but Balassa (1973, p. 357) cites evidence that the industrial associations in Hungary have encountered diseconomies of scale in management.

Another purpose of the consolidations was improvement in the process of technological development. In cases where an association includes a research institute as well as production facilities, better coordination should develop between the two. Under the prior organizational structure, research was often not directed towards the needs of production, and technological advances were often not put to use. It was also suggested that associations would be better able to handle foreign trade than either the ministry (which is not sufficiently close to enterprise import needs and export abilities) or the enterprise itself (which may be too small to have much bargaining power). In most of the socialist countries, economies of scale in export selling had previously been achieved by concentrating all foreign trade in a single import–export firm for each industry. The associations were given the right to deal directly with foreign firms, since their size made it practical for them to do so.

One of the most important expected benefits of the mergers was economies of scale in production. Clearly the merger of several enterprises producing similar products may have this effect, although when they remain physically separate, as was often the case, the benefits are less certain. What is interesting is that the greatest economies of scale are likely to result from *vertical* integration. Because of the extreme uncertainties of supply, socialist enterprises have traditionally devoted a great deal of material and labor resources to producing their own inputs. For example, Balassa (1981, p. 30n) tells us that large Hungarian manufacturers of final goods make 90 per cent of their own tools. Similarly, Soviet lifting and transporting equipment is produced by 320 different enterprises, of which 250 are making it for their own use. Only 14 per cent is made by the ministry responsible for supplying it to others. Also, only 41 per cent of Soviet computers, 32 per cent of plastic products and 67 per cent of forging presses are made by the ministries that are supposed to supply them. (Gorlin, 1976a, p. 169; Smolinski, 1974, p. 29). Thus vertical integration with an enterprise that will reliably supply some input should free another enterprise to specialize in the product it is supposed to produce.

In more general terms, the advantage of vertical integration in a planned economy is that the central planners are freed from the need to coordinate and supervise production of intermediate products. Instead of formulating output targets and success criteria for each of several stages of production, only the final results need be appraised. It was largely for this reason that many of the socialist associations were created by mergers that were primarily vertical. This was especially true in Bulgaria, Czechoslovakia, East Germany, Poland and Romania,[5] but occurred to some extent in every country.

The existence of these vertically integrated organizations raises some fundamental questions. If mergers are horizontal, they may create firms that are very large in terms of number of employees, assets or value of output, but still relatively uncomplicated in terms of the problems of coordinating different economic activities. But when successive stages in the production process are carried out within the same firm, the question arises of how to coordinate those processes. In particular, the question arises of the appropriate extent of autonomy for the constituent subunits.

Autonomy of Subunits
The associations were to be given a considerable amount of independence from the central planners. Indeed, that is the essential, novel feature of their creation. But also very interesting is the fact that in some cases the enterprises comprising the associations were supposed to retain some autonomy. Thus, there is an obvious parallel with

Yugoslav firms, which are independent of central planners and at the same time consist of autonomous divisions. The degree of independence of the subunits of the associations varies all the way from the complete autonomy of Hungarian enterprises (for whom membership in the associations was voluntary[6]) to the thorough subordination of East German and Bulgarian enterprises to their associations. In the Soviet Union, Poland and Romania there are cases where the members of an association retain a considerable degree of autonomy, including their own bank accounts and separate profit and loss accounting; but many enterprises in those countries lost all or part of their autonomy when the association was formed. In Czechoslovakia and Bulgaria, the member enterprises originally had substantial independence but changes in the system (in 1969 in Czechoslovakia and in 1971 in Bulgaria) have deprived them of it. However, according to Gorlin (1974, p. 530) in the early 1970s 'the trend in Eastern Europe . . . [was that] the enterprise [was] gaining increased authority at the expense of the association'. Blazyca (1980, p. 320) claims that most Polish associations (the so-called Big Enterprises) are highly centralized, but he admits that a study of twelve of them showed that, in four, 'member enterprises enjoy a significant degree of decentralization'.

The autonomy of the enterprises that form the socialist associations can be measured in a number of dimensions. Perhaps most important is the *khozraschet* status. Like a division in a Yugoslav firm, an economic unit on *khozraschet* maintains separate bookkeeping, has its own bank accounts and has legal authority to make financial commitments. Further, it is expected to cover all of its costs from its own revenue, to repay bank loans and to earn a profit. Member enterprises have *khozraschet* status in some (but not all) industrial associations in the Soviet Union, Hungary, Romania, Bulgaria (1963–1971 only) and Czechoslovakia (until 1970) (Hohmann *et al.*, 1975, pp. 183–4; Marczewski, 1974, p. 83; Zielinski, 1973, p. 286). In some cases (especially in East Germany), member enterprises are judged (and bonuses are paid) in part on the basis of profit earned, despite extensive interference in their operations by the association (Keren, 1973, p. 143; Marczewski, 1974, pp. 86–8). This conflicts with a basic principle of western business practice that states that a subdivision should not be held responsible for profit when its control over the variables that determine profit is limited (Dearden, 1962, Solomons, 1965, p. 3).

Other dimensions of autonomy concern the right of the association to make investment decisions and to redistribute inputs, capital and profits among member enterprises. Practice varies widely in these dimensions and is not always correlated with *khozraschet* status.

In some cases the organizational structure is complex: subunits may be partially independent of the association but nevertheless be responsive to certain instructions directly from the central planning board. In this case, the purpose of creating the association has been defeated. There should be logical rules on which type of decisions are to be made at each level. For example, shop floor organization could be decided by the subunits, major production targets at the association level, and investment allocation (how much money but not exactly which machines, etc.) by the ministry. But if the central planners send instructions directly to the subunits of the association, then they are devoting time to what can be done better by others. Gorlin (1974, p. 528) claims that this happens often in the Soviet Union because the ministries are reluctant to relinquish their control.

Effect of the Associations on Transactional Efficiency

In the remainder of this chapter I examine the impact on transactional efficiency of the organizational changes embodied in the creation of the socialist associations. If we agree with Oliver Williamson that in most circumstances transaction costs are substantial, then it is evident that these changes can have an important impact.

Williamson does not explicitly deal with planned economies;[7] his emphasis is on the fact that bounded rationality and opportunism can interfere with contracts and hence under certain circumstances it is more efficient to substitute administrative control for the market mechanism. But he does discuss (1975, chapters 7 and 8) the situation where a firm gets so large that it can benefit from divisionalization. In this form, his analysis is quite appropriate for application to the socialist countries, where attention has focused on the choice not between market and administrative coordinating mechanisms, but between what we might call local and central administrative control.

To divisionalize means to create subunits. Usually, this involves breaking up some organization into small pieces, but in this case the opposite is happening: smaller units (enterprises) are being merged to form associations. Either way the principle is the same: the socialist associations, like enterprises in the West, result from a process described by Coase (1937), that is, the cost of decision-making and economic coordination within some organization is weighed against the cost of some external mechanism. In the West, that external mechanism is a market; in the Soviet-type economies, the alternative to putting transactions into the firm is leaving them to the central planners. But in both cases the decision whether or not to put more transactions inside an economic unit is largely a matter of transaction costs. An essential feature of organizational development in the socialist countries over the last two decades is the effort to reduce costs by creating an economic unit that encompasses more transactions.

Similarities with organizational structures in western firms (i.e. multidivisional form) suggest that this is a step in the direction of greater transactional efficiency.

Bounded Rationality and Opportunism

Many of the problems that led to the major economic reforms in the socialist countries can be viewed as problems of bounded rationality and opportunism. In their efforts to run 'the whole of society . . . [as] one office and one factory', the socialist planners encountered the limits to their own ability to absorb and process information, and hence the limit to their ability to make efficiently either day-to-day decisions or basic long-run policy decisions. In describing the excessive growth of large capitalist enterprises, Alfred Chandler and Oliver Williamson make statements that fit the centrally planned systems quite well:

> . . . the administrative load on the senior executives increased to such an extent that they were unable to handle their entrepreneurial responsibilities efficiently. This situation arose when the operations of the enterprise became too complex and the problems of coordination, appraisal, and policy formulation too intricate for a small number of top officers to handle both long-run, entrepreneurial, and short-run, operational administrative activities. (Chandler, 1966, pp. 382–3)

> Continued expansion also eventually overcomes the capacity of the office of the chief executive to provide strategic planning and maintain effective control, which is another manifestation of bounded rationality. (Williamson, 1975, p. 135)

The same bounded rationality interferes with the relationship between socialist central planners and the directors of enterprises: contractual incompleteness, which is normally thought of as a problem of the market mechanism, is also a problem for the central planners, who cannot completely specify what they want from each enterprise. The traditional problems of assortment and quality are the most obvious examples of this. The situation can be described as a set of incomplete contracts (the central planners cannot specify all the relevant details), with opportunistic behavior by enterprise managers leading to socially inefficient behavior. An illustration is given by the well-known Soviet cartoon showing a firm that has met its monthly production quota for nails by making one enormous nail. Putting the nail manufacturer and user of nails together in an association reduces the problem.

Even if associations are formed by horizontal mergers, transaction cost benefits can result. Sharing or trading inputs is subject to opportunistic behavior no less than supplying intermediate goods, especially since much of it is ad hoc, outside of official channels and hence not enforceable in courts. What is needed to insure efficient implementation of agreements to share or trade inputs is a nearby superior who can threaten to punish opportunistic behavior.

The problem is that the contractual relationship governing directors' remuneration does not encourage efficient decision-making: as long as their own earnings depend on meeting targets that cannot be fully specified, they do not have the proper incentives. It has long been recognized that managers of socialist enterprises pursue narrow goals that differ from those of the central planners. Speaking of the capitalist firm, Williamson says (1975, p. 135) that, if managers perceive a situation

> ... as affording them with opportunities for discretion, because information is impacted to their advantage, and if, in addition, managers are given to behave opportunistically, further consequences obtain. Deliberate distortions will be introduced into the hierarchical information exchange process in support of subgoals. Permissive attitudes toward slack may also develop.

This sounds very familiar to any student of the planned economies.

Another observation of Williamson's regarding opportunism fits the ministers in the Soviet-type economies: he says (1975, p. 135) that often firms decide

> ... to bring the heads of the functional divisions into the peak coordination process. The natural posture for these functional executives to take is one of advocacy in representing the interests of their respective operating units.

For many years ministers in the socialist economies have been known to have narrow perspective and to be primarily concerned with the prestige and growth of their own domains.

Multidivisional Structure

The capitalist firms' response to these problems has been to shift from a single unified hierarchy (unitary form) to a structure of at least partially autonomous operating divisions (multidivisional form). As discussed in chapter 1, their reason for doing so is usually to reduce the center's loss of control in two ways: (1) by correcting faulty or incomplete information flows, both up and down the hierarchy, and (2) by restricting the pursuit of subgoals by various parts of the enterprise. The very same reason can be adduced for the changes in the industrial organization of the socialist countries. Chandler's description (1966, pp. 382–3) of the success that led to the widespread adoption of multidivisional form among capitalist firms would be very appealing to the socialist proponents of the creation of industrial associations:

> The basic reason for its success was simply that it clearly removed the executives responsible for the destiny of the entire enterprise from the more routine operational activities, and so gave them the time, information, and even psychological commitment for long-term planning and appraisal . . .
> [The] new structure left the broad strategic decisions as to the allocation of existing resources and the acquisition of new ones in the hands of a top team . . .

This separation of broad strategic decision-making from daily operating decisions is the essence of multidivisional structure. It necessarily implies extensive delegation to autonomous subdivisions of authority to make operating decisions. For this reason, the Soviet reform of 1965 was not a true transition to multidivisional form, since many ministries subsequently violated the rules by interfering in the daily operations of the associations and even enterprises under their jurisdiction. Equally, the more recent creation of associations in the Soviet Union and similar changes in Eastern Europe are only a half step in the direction of multidivisional structure because the scope of authority yielded to the association is so restricted. Nonetheless, the step is clearly in that direction.

But it should be clear that multidivisional form does not mean total and unqualified independence for the divisions. On the contrary, Williamson tells us that this form was developed primarily in order to overcome the problems of loss of control by the center and pursuit of goals other than profit by lower levels of the hierarchy. Therefore, he puts great emphasis (for example, 1975, pp. 137–8) on the advisory and auditing functions of the center, both of which improve its control over the divisions. In the socialist economy, by freeing the center from routine tasks, the new system should allow it to overcome information impactedness and to develop fine-tuning techniques so that its control over the important macro variables is improved and so that opportunistic behavior by enterprise managers is reduced.

It is important to make explicit the fact that with Williamson's multidivisional structure the center does retain important functions. In particular, it is the center that does the long-term planning, that allocates major resources among the divisions and that appraises the performance of the divisions, distributing rewards as it deems appropriate. Thus, what Williamson had in mind could be, in some cases, said to fit either the relationship between the ministry and the association or the relationship between the association and its constituent enterprises.

Transaction Characteristics
Given the socialist countries' decision to transfer some information processing and decision-making to lower levels of the hierarchy, a major question is that of deciding how to break up the monolithic structure, that is, where to draw the dividing lines between the divisions. Here Williamson's analysis is particularly appropriate. He defines (1979, pp. 239 and 261) governance structures as 'the institutional matrix within which transactions are negotiated and executed', and tells us that efficiency depends on matching governance structures with the attributes of the transactions that must be executed. He specifies three critical dimensions of transactions that must be considered when choosing an appropriate governance structure: (1) the frequency with which transactions recur; (2) the amount of uncertainty involved; and (3) the degree to which durable transaction-specific investments (human or physical) are incurred. To the extent that the socialist associations are designed to reflect these criteria, they will improve the efficiency of the economy by reducing overall transaction costs.

In terms of the frequency with which transactions recur, it is clear that the creation of associations is a step towards greater efficiency. Enterprises whose relationship is such that they must repeatedly interact are brought together in a single organization. Whether the association is a horizontal merger of enterprises that must share common inputs or a vertical merger of enterprises that must continually negotiate the details of the design and delivery of intermediate products, the fact that they are subject to unified administrative command reduces many of the transaction costs that would accompany either longer administrative lines of command or market negotiations. In the case of an association consisting of a number of horizontally related enterprises (which use similar inputs and/or produce similar outputs), the most obvious reduction in transaction costs comes from jointly arranging for supplies and low-cost shuffling of supplies among members. If one enterprise needs something that another has in excess, there need be neither a market contract nor transmission of request and command all the way to Moscow and back. A similar reduction in transmission of information comes from having the association director, rather than a more distant planner, assign and, when necessary, redistribute output targets, in terms of both quantities and assortments.

In designing vertical associations, too, the key consideration is the frequency of transactions. Obviously, one could argue for including under common control an entire process from mining raw materials to distributing final products. This is the principle that led to the creation of the original ministries. But the idea of the associations is to be more selective, and frequency of transactions is perhaps the most important of the criteria for deciding which vertical stages to group together. If the characteristics, qualities, time and manner of delivery of an intermediate product can be settled, say, annually, then there is less need to group supplier and user together. If, on the other hand, quantities and characteristics of the intermediate product must be adjusted, say, weekly or monthly, then the transaction cost advantage of having local administrative control is greater.

A second major consideration when choosing the structure that will govern a set of transactions is uncertainty. If at the time of a transaction the needs and abilities of two enterprises can be known with some confidence, then the relationship between them (for example, one will deliver to the other a particular quantity of a certain product) can be established by the central planners without much avoidable transaction cost. However, if the transaction inevitably involves uncertainty (for example, if ability to deliver depends on the weather or if the users' specifications cannot be known in advance), then the advantage of local administrative control over central control is greater. For example, a construction enterprise cannot know in advance the quantity and type of concrete it will need on a particular day. By assigning it to an association that includes a cement factory, the cost of coordination can be substantially reduced.

The third of Williamson's transactions characteristics is the extent to which a transaction involves investment that is durable and specific to a particular customer or supplier. Often this is a matter of physical proximity: if two enterprises are located adjacent to one another, and if transportation cost, the danger of spoilage or, say, heat retention of an intermediate product is important, then, all other things being equal, there is a stronger case for combining them in an association. Regardless of location, if an enterprise has to acquire machinery or build a whole plant in order to supply a specific user, and could not switch that capital to alternative users (or could do so only after expensive modifications), then again there is reason to combine supplier and user. It might also be the user, rather than the supplier, who makes the specific investment that suggests that two enterprises be put into the same association. For example, a smelter may be built to process a particular type or grade of ore, an aluminum products fabricator may rely on ingots or sheets that are available from only one domestic refinery, or a plastics maker may be able to use the output of only one domestic petrochemical plant. It is also possible that it is human capital that is transaction-specific and thus ties one enterprise to another. That is, it may be highly trained employees, not machinery, who enable an enterprise to provide or use some intermediate product.

It should be clear that these three characteristics of transactions are not, either individually or as a group, sufficient reason to combine enterprises into an association. Each is a matter of degree and to some extent will apply in many, if not most, cases. They are factors to be weighed in deciding where to draw the dividing lines in grouping enterprises, given the decision to relieve the center of some of the burden of planning.

Evidence on the extent to which the socialist countries have been guided by these considerations in their formation of associations is scanty. There are reports of some apparently illogical mergers, but most appear to fit the criteria. Furthermore, Williamson's characteristics make clear that factors other than physical proximity can be important. Hence some of the western criticism of mergers of widely separated enterprises may be unwarranted.

Summary

When talking about the planned economies in terms of multidivisional structure, it is sometimes appropriate to think of the associations as consisting of several divisions, and sometimes more appropriate to treat the associations as themselves being divisions of a ministry. But either way (and sometimes both ways), the creation of associations can have important advantages in terms of transaction efficiency. By bringing transactions inside an association, problems of bounded rationality and opportunism are reduced and thus some of the costs of using a planning mechanism are lowered.

Development of the associations can be seen as an organizational analog to the international diffusion of technology: just as technological advances made in one country gradually spread to others, so too organizational forms that have transaction cost advantages over other forms can spread from one country to another. The structural changes described in this chapter can be viewed as a form of organizational diffusion: the socialist countries are adopting structures, already in use in other countries, that they see as useful. There are, of course, important differences between the socialist associations and capitalist or Yugoslav multidivisional corporations; they are not abandoning their fundamental principles. But there are important similarities, too. It is

142 Self-Management and Efficiency: Large Corporations in Yugoslavia

not very remarkable that the idea of multidivisional structure spread from the United States to Western Europe. It is more interesting that it is evident in contemporary Yugoslav enterprise structure. But what is most surprising is that the same fundamental concept shows signs of taking hold in the planned economies of Eastern Europe and the Soviet Union. The same search for efficiency and rationality that leads capitalist enterprises to choose certain organizational structures leads system designers in socialist countries to impose similar structures on their own enterprises.

Notes

1 These quotations from Lenin are from 'Political Report of the Central Committee', 7 March, 1918 and *State and Revolution* and are cited in Roberts (1971), pp. 29, 10n and 28.
2 Statistics on Eastern European associations are taken from the following sources: Keren (1973), pp. 137–9; Marczewski (1974), pp. 73, 89 and 91; Granick (1975a), pp. 37, 38 and 40; Hohmann *et al.* (1975), p. 96; Blazyca (1980), p. 321; Balassa (1981), pp. 28–9. For further discussion of the associations see also Kaser and Zielinski (1970), pp. 42–4; Pryor (1973), pp. 217–22; Marczewski (1974), pp. 83–97; Nuti (1977); Bornstein (1977), pp. 113–14.
3 Statistics on Soviet enterprises and associations are taken from the following sources: Smolinski (1974), pp. 24–5; Lavigne (1975), p. 77; Gorlin (1976a), pp. 162–4 and 168; Schroeder (1979), p. 316. See also Green (1977).
4 Actually, the concept of associations goes back to 1929, but in this context we need not trace it back that far. See Katz (1972), p. 17.
5 Hohmann *et al.* (1975), pp. 96 and 183; Holesovsky (1973), p. 342; Keren (1973), pp. 139 and 141; Marczewski (1974), pp. 72–5; Pryor (1973), pp. 225–8; Spigler (1973), p. 63. By contrast, Schrenk *et al.* (1979), pp. 58 and 60n, claim that, except for Yugoslavia, the East European associations were formed 'almost exclusively' by horizontal mergers.
6 However, many Hungarian enterprises are themselves the result of earlier mergers. Subunits of the enterprises (as opposed to the associations of enterprises) do not have independence.
7 'The alternative organizational modes examined here are strictly firm and market; central planning boards never expressly enter the picture' (Williamson, 1975, p. 5).

8 Summary

For decades Yugoslavia has been viewed as a laboratory where a series of variations on the economic system of self-management are tried out. Since the 1960s there have been two major trends, which might appear to conflict with one another: (1) increasing autonomy for small work units, and (2) various schemes intended to result in greater coordination among separate economic units. These trends pervade the entire economy, but are most evident within large enterprises. Together, they raise a question that is fundamental to our understanding of both the Yugoslav economy in particular and organizational alternatives in general: is the existence of large firms compatible with meaningful implementation of the principle of self-management? The Yugoslav response to this apparent conflict is to divisionalize firms, that is, to create a system of enterprise subunits. This in turn leads to the issue of the efficiency of that organizational structure.

Some observers claim that the autonomy of Yugoslav divisions is exaggerated and that the central administration of the enterprise exercises *de facto* control. But I argue in chapter 1 that their independence is quite real and that they do buy and sell goods and services among themselves. The increasing independence of divisions is a continuation of a trend in Yugoslavia that goes back to 1950. During the following two decades, enterprises became increasingly independent of Belgrade and during the third decade (the 1970s) *divisions* became increasingly independent of their own enterprise headquarters. The constitutional amendments of 1971, the Constitution of 1974 and the Law on Associated Labor of 1976 codified divisional autonomy. By law, each separately identifiable activity must be organized as an independent division. Obviously, such a law is not easily implemented, but virtually every enterprise has attempted to do so, with varying results. In general, divisions tend to consist of 300–400 workers and vary in range of activities from quite narrow to rather broad (the latter being in cases where a division encompasses all the activities connected with production of a single product).

Within enterprises, the relationship among divisions approaches a market relationship: independent economic entities exchange goods and services for money at prices negotiated between them. These transfer prices are not set by enterprise headquarters, and are generally close to the corresponding prices on external markets. This is largely because the divisions have the freedom to buy and sell outside the firm, a freedom that is important even if not often exercised. If prices or conditions for transactions within the enterprise were less favorable than those obtainable outside, one division or the other would not agree to the transaction. Of course, in many cases non-price aspects of a transaction (e.g. delivery time or reliability) are decisive, but that does not mean that it is not a market transaction.

For many intermediate products there is no readily available outside market price. In that case (and sometimes even when a market price *is* available) the transfer price results from negotiations among divisions about the distribution of the revenue from the sale of a final product. But those percentages that are negotiated may be no less prices than if they were stated in absolute amounts: in some cases the only difference is that an element of uncertainty is introduced by the fact that the expected transfer of money may be scaled up or down. Of course, if transfer prices are set *after* production decisions are made, the former can influence the latter only with a lag. Regardless of whether the transfer price is stated in terms of absolute amounts or percentages of expected total revenue, neither division will for long accept a price that it thinks is worse than it could get by dealing with others (or even by withdrawing from the firm). That is, transfer prices will reflect their perceptions of long-run market alternatives.

One of the major advantages of divisionalization, if transfer prices are meaningful, is the information it provides for evaluating the performance of particular activities. That is, it facilitates rational decisions about which activities to expand and which to abandon. Of course, the transfer prices do not always reflect all of the costs and benefits; sometimes there are externalities that demand continuation or expansion of an apparently unprofitable activity. But the basic principle, which is generally respected, is that transfer prices should include such costs and benefits. In those cases where a firm decides to continue to operate a division despite recurring losses, a subsidy is in effect drawn from the rest of the enterprise. Thus, a claim that there is such an externality must be explicit, quantified and justified. Without the requirement that each activity constitute a separate division with its own accounting, such explicit information might not be available.

It is clear that, despite the autonomy of its subunits, the Yugoslav enterprise is a meaningful economic unit. A strong sense of solidarity binds together the divisions of an enterprise and they will in some cases honor and renew contracts that are not advantageous in a narrow sense. This is partly a matter of Party and social pressure to deal with sister divisions and partly a matter of choosing long-term stability over short-term profits. The unity of the firm is particularly evident in those cases where transfer prices are stated in terms of a percentage share of final sales. To a large extent, the enterprise takes its significance from the capital flows within it. These may take the form of fixed-interest loans or joint projects that earn variable returns. Capital flows are part of the joint planning that ties together the constituent parts of the firm. In fact, joint activities in some cases result in *de facto* creation of a firm. The fact of joint planning among a group of divisions is not an operational definition of the Yugoslav enterprise because planning and joint investment can be, and often are, undertaken by divisions that are *not* in the same enterprise. But if joint activities are handled in the manner characteristic of Yugoslav firms, as discussed in chapter 4, then the divisions involved have in effect formed an enterprise.

One might not expect to find large corporations in Yugoslavia because it is an economic system based on the principle of self-management by small work units. Jaroslav Vanek and others predicted that labor-managed firms would be *smaller* than capitalist firms. But, contrary to theoretical predictions, the evidence shows that in fact Yugoslav firms do experience an impetus to grow, to control a sizable portion of their industries, and even to expand into other industries. Chapter 2 shows that giant firms and conglomerates are numerous in Yugoslavia and that they account for a large and growing share of economic activity. Some firms employ tens of thousands of workers. This growth of firms raises questions about the feasibility of relying on competitive markets to ensure economic efficiency, about the viability of the principle of self-management and about the efficiency of the organizational structure of Yugoslav firms.

Chapter 2 begins by examining several reasons for believing that firm size is important to the operation of market socialism. Its central argument is that large firms do exist in Yugoslavia and may have competitive advantages over smaller firms, advantages that are not always based on true economic costs. The existence of these advantages may reduce the competitive pressure that a market system relies on to keep each firm's cost near its minimum and price near cost. Large size is important not only relative to a firm's own market but also relative to all other firms. Large absolute size can confer advantages in gaining access to capital and can be used to win customers through reciprocal buying agreements. To the extent that such advantages are merely pecuniary and do not reflect any real economies, they interfere with the proper functioning of the market.

Of course, the vitality of competition is not determined entirely by the size of the competitors. But the Yugoslav economy is primarily a market system and the performance of a market is at least influenced by the size and number of participants. Also influenced is the dispersion of decision-making power: the replacement of a large number of small firms by a few large ones could mean the concentration of economic power in the hands of relatively few people. Indeed, the data do show what Vanek might call 'inordinate concentrations of industrial power'.

Data that deal not with whole enterprises but with divisions show quite a different picture. It appears that during the 1970s there was an *increase* in the number of actors and a *decrease* in the variance of their size distribution. Particularly evident is an increase in the number of units with under 500 workers and a single specific activity. On this basis the prospects for effective competition and dispersion of economic power look brighter, but a lot depends on the relationship between divisions. There is reason to believe that there is more market sharing and price fixing within corporations than between them.

Chapter 3 examines one aspect of the relationship between the divisions of a self-managed enterprise, namely, transfer prices. The major point is that transfer prices between divisions can have an important impact on the allocation of resources in a self-managed socialist economy. Of course, if the central administration of the enterprise exercises effective control over all or most of the firm's economic activities, then transfer prices may serve merely an accounting function. But if the divisions are truly independent, then transfer prices do affect the efficiency of input and output decisions.

Furthermore, if the divisions are autonomous, there is a real danger of misallocation. This is due primarily to the fact that labor is not treated as a commodity to be bought and sold: a division may choose not to take on more workers even though there are people (perhaps other workers in the same firm) willing to supply labor in return for an income level lower than the division's current marginal productivity. That is, there may be immobility of labor between divisions where marginal productivity is high and divisions where it is low. However, something equivalent to the reallocation of labor between divisions can be achieved if, as shown in chapters 1 and 6, one division buys services from another. Of course, inputs other than labor can be sold between divisions, too. Thus, misallocation can be corrected by the proper use of interdivisional transfer prices.

Perhaps the most important question dealt with in this study is whether the extensive divisionalization of Yugoslav firms reduces efficiency by defeating the very purpose of creating firms. That is, has implementation of the principles of self-management by small work units led to excessive fragmentation of the enterprise? In trying to answer this question we should keep in mind the fact that, in countries where the law does not require independent subunits, many enterprises have *chosen* to divisionalize. That is certainly true in the United

States. Thus it seems safe to say that that structure is not inefficient in principle; rather, the question is whether the Yugoslavs have carried the idea too far.

The transactions cost analysis in chapter 4 suggests that the answer to this question depends on the relationship among the divisions. Williamson tells us that the efficiency advantage of bringing transactions into the firm rather than leaving them to the market lies in the fact that this solves the problem of contractual incompleteness: that is, bounded rationality makes it impossible to specify contracts completely and opportunism makes incomplete contracts hazardous and possibly socially inefficient. To the extent that the unity or solidarity of the Yugoslav firm reduces opportunistic behavior, independent divisions can coordinate their activities with long-term contracts, despite the contractual incompleteness that is inevitable because of bounded rationality. Because opportunistic behavior is reduced, sharing clauses can be written into contracts to allow the adaptive, sequential decision-making that constitutes the major reason for creating firms. That is, technologically separate activities can relate to one another through a market mechanism because the firm constitutes a shell within which incomplete contracts do not pose a threat. Inside that shell, more complicated and longer-term coordination can be governed by a market mechanism without the transactions cost inefficiencies that would result from the more opportunistic behavior encountered outside the firm. In other words, the fragmentation of the Yugoslav enterprise will not lead to inefficiency (will not be excessive) if the behavior of the divisions is not opportunistic. The strong sense of enterprise solidarity described in chapters 1 and 6 suggests at least a reduction, if not total elimination, of opportunistic behavior.

Chapter 5 deals with investment decisions in the divisionalized Yugoslav firm. It examines some theoretical questions in order to set the stage for chapter 6, which contains case studies of the structure of large corporations. After looking at the well-known Furubotn/Pejovich bias, which explains workers' reluctance to invest in their own firm, it points out that inflation may cause an opposite bias, that is, a worker preference for investment in the real assets of the firm rather than the monetary assets of individual savings.

The most important question dealt with in this chapter is whether divisionalization has any effect on the amount of investment undertaken by the firm. The theoretical literature suggests that workers are more willing to invest with borrowed money than with their own savings or with retained corporate profits. A plausible argument can be made that, within a divisionalized enterprise, each subunit would treat loans from another subunit as outside credit and hence be willing to invest more than if the firm were not divisionalized. However, this argument breaks down when we look at the limitations on divisions' willingness to engage in either borrowing or lending. Of prime importance is a fact often overlooked in the published literature: the willingness to invest with borrowed money depends heavily on the time duration of the loan. Because an investment decision cannot be reversed, outside funding will not by itself induce workers to undertake a project if the loan must be paid off very soon. The length of time to which the lender will agree depends on his expectations regarding alternative investment opportunities.

Much of the analysis in this chapter hinges on a fundamental institutional characteristic of the Yugoslav system, namely, the firm's obligation to maintain the value of its capital. We might expect there to be situations where a division is more willing to lend to a sister division than to invest directly in physical assets for itself because it would thereby avoid any commitment to future outlays; someone else would be responsible for making depreciation payments for the eventual replacement of physical assets. That is, a financial asset (the debt of another division) has a zero rate of depreciation. However, the Yugoslav rule that repayment of principle must go into the lender's business fund means that money loaned out cannot later be distributed for consumption. Therefore, workers will be induced to lend only if they expect a rate of return equal to the same critical rate necessary to induce them to invest in their own division. There does not seem, then, to be any reason to expect divisionalization per se to affect the amount the firm invests.

Of course, this does not mean that there will be no interdivisional lending. If a firm or part of a firm is given an opportunity to earn a higher rate of return by lending than it could earn by investing directly in physical assets for its own use or by putting the money in a bank, it may choose to lend (depending on liquidity and risk). If money has already accumulated in its business fund, the lender will be seeking the highest return it can get. If not, and if the prospective return is high enough, the lending division's workers may be willing to contribute funds from their own savings or from additional retained earnings.

There are also other explanations for interdivisional lending that are not encompassed by the theory of investment. For example, there may be pressure to help modernize a backward sister division. Chapter 6 takes a more empirical approach and shows that interdivisional and interfirm capital flows often result from a need for a particular input, as well as from a simple search for high rates of return. In the cases examined, firms undertake projects that would not have been realized in the absence of interdivisional lending.

In some of these cases it is difficult to know whether the divisions are in the same firm or not. But the fact that their agreements provide for joint business councils and include income-sharing clauses suggests that for practical purposes they are. Further, they demonstrate a willingness to operate with contractual incompleteness: the joint management boards allow adaptive, sequential decision-making. Apparently, the participants in these cases believe that opportunistic behavior is not a serious problem.

In each case, the search for profits is made quite explicit, as is the lenders' willingness to tie up funds for as long as fifteen years. Unfortunately, it is not possible to know whether borrowers are willing to enter such agreements because they anticipate rates of return higher than the critical r discussed in chapter 5 or because they view the repayment period as extending beyond their time horizon (that is, because they see the burden of paying for the project as falling on future workers). But since in every case repayment is in installments beginning rather soon, at least some of the burden falls within the time horizon of most present workers.

Some cases can be viewed in terms of the analysis in chapter 3: by buying goods and services from one another, the divisions are in effect reallocating labor; that is, workers in one division are essentially working for another division.

The major problem of joint activity among divisions is measuring each division's contribution and thus its proper share of income. In some cases this is a fairly straightforward matter of negotiating a transfer price for intermediate goods. In other cases there is a more complicated procedure for dividing up the revenue from the sale of a final product. But the results must be approximately the same because if the final distribution of income were substantially different from the participants' estimates of market prices, then one side or the other would withdraw or insist on a readjustment. That is, if the producer (or buyer) of an intermediate good thought he could do better by operating independently and selling (or buying) his product on the market (either to the same user (supplier) or to others), he would do so. Of course, sometimes there is no established outside market to look to for comparable prices. But it is always possible for a division to estimate how well it would do out on its own.

An important question is whether transfer prices affect the allocation of resources. In some of the cases, transfer prices are determined exogenously and production decisions seem to be based on those prices. In other cases, transfer prices seem to be set *after* production decisions are made and hence are primarily a device for distributing income. However, to the extent that production decisions are made with last year's prices in mind, there may be a lagged effect.

An interesting aspect of some of the cases described in chapter 6 is the fact that they make very clear that some workers are residual claimants only in a limited way. Those who work directly with jointly financed facilities receive personal incomes and collective consumption on a level tied to that of the workers who contribute funds to the project. Because the residual, after some predetermined level of incomes is subtracted, is shared by both groups (those who finance and those who work with the facilities), the risk is shared. The income of each group depends on the success of the other. In these circumstances, the contribution of capital (which the Yugoslavs call 'past labor') constitutes a basis for income distribution: a group of workers with money to lend can use that money to earn money, not only by investing at a fixed rate of return but also by accepting a variable return that is determined by the success of another activity.

The purpose of chapter 7 is to show that many of the basic concepts used in earlier chapters are also relevant to other socialist countries. For much of the past two decades the Soviet Union and most East European countries have experimented with changes in the size of their basic economic units and with the administrative organizational structure of enterprises. They, too, are clearly concerned with reconciling the two trends noted at the beginning of chapter 8, namely, greater decision-making power for small economic units and efficient mechanisms for coordinating their activities. The concepts of optimal firm size, divisionalization and transactions cost used in this book have implications for the efficiency of the associations, trusts, etc. that have been created in the Soviet Union and Eastern Europe.

Like western firms, these socialist associations result from a process of weighing the cost of decision-making within an economic unit against the cost of using some external mechanism. In Yugoslavia and the West, that external mechanism is a market and in the Soviet-type system the alternative to putting transactions inside the enterprise is leaving them to the central planners. But in both cases a major concern is the reduction of transaction costs. The creation of these associations reflects the view of those in charge of the economic systems of these socialist countries that a more efficient way to coordinate certain activities is to move them into an organizational unit in which they will be partially insulated from detailed instructions from outside. Thus, the association constitutes a shell within which transactions are handled differently, perhaps by negotiations between individual sub-units. Such a development could be viewed as international diffusion of organizational structure: in their search for efficiency and rationality, the socialist countries are choosing organizational structures that have certain similarities to the multidivisional form that has already been adopted by western and Yugoslav firms.

References

Alchian, Armen A. and Harold Demsetz (1972), 'Production information costs and economic organization', *American Economic Review*, 62, 5 (December), pp. 777–95.

Arrow, Kenneth J. (1964), 'Control in large organizations', *Management Science*, 10, 3 (April), pp. 397–408.

Arrow, Kenneth J. (1969), 'The organization of economic activity', in *The Analysis and Evaluation of Public Expenditure: The PPB System* (Washington, DC: Joint Economic Committee, 91st Congress, 1st Session), pp. 59–73.

Atkinson, A. B. (1973), 'Worker management and the modern industrial enterprise', *Quarterly Journal of Economics*, 87, 3 (August), pp. 375–92.

Atkinson, A. B. (1975), 'Worker management and the modern industrial enterprise: a reply', *Quarterly Journal of Economics*, 89, 4 (November), pp. 670–2.

Balassa, Bela (1973), 'The firm in the new economic mechanism in Hungary', in Morris Bornstein (ed.), *Plan and Market* (New Haven, Conn.: Yale University Press).

Balassa, Bela (1981), 'Reforming the new economic mechanism in Hungary', mimeo, presented to the American Economic Association, Washington, DC, December.

Baumol, William and Tibor Fabian (1964), 'Decomposition, pricing for decentralization, and external economies', *Management Science*, 11, 1 (September), pp. 1–32.

Berle, Adolf and Gardiner Means (1932), *The Modern Corporation and Private Property* (New York, NY: Macmillan).

Bernstein, Paul (1976), *Workplace Democratization: Its Internal Dynamics* (Kent, Ohio: Kent State University Press).

Blazyca, G. (1980), 'Industrial structure and the economic problems of industry in a centrally planned economy: the Polish case', *Journal of Industrial Economics*, 28, 3 (March), pp. 313–26.

Blumberg, Paul (1968), *Industrial Democracy: The Sociology of Participation* (New York: Schocken).

Booth, E. J. R. and Oscar W. Jensen (1977), 'Transfer prices in the global corporation under internal and external constraints', *Canadian Journal of Economics*, 10, 3 (August), pp. 434–46.

Bornstein, Morris (1977), 'Economic reform in Eastern Europe', in *East European Economies Post-Helsinki* (Washington, DC: US Congress Joint Economic Committee, 25 August), pp. 102–34.

Braverman, Harry (1974), *Labor and Monopoly Capital: The Degradation of Work in the Twentieth Century* (New York, NY: Monthly Review Press).

Bulletin, published weekly by the Yugoslav Press and Cultural Center, New York.

Buttrick, John (1952), 'The inside contract system', *Journal of Economic History*, 12, 3 (Summer), pp. 205–21.

Chandler, Alfred (1966), *Strategy and Structure* (Cambridge, Mass.: MIT Press and New York, NY: Doubleday and Co., Anchor Books Edition).

Chernoff, H. and L. E. Moses (1959), *Elementary Decision Theory* (New York, NY: John Wiley & Sons).

Cheung, Steven (1983), 'The contractual nature of the firm', *Journal of Law and Economics*, 26, 1 (April), pp. 1–21.

Coase, Ronald H. (1937), 'The nature of the firm', *Economica*, 4, 16 (November), pp. 386–405.

Coase, Ronald H. (1960), 'The problem of social cost', *Journal of Law and Economics*, 3 (October), pp 1–44.

Comisso, Ellen Turkish (1979), *Workers' Control Under Plan and Market* (New Haven, Conn.: Yale University Press).

Comisso, Ellen T. (1980), 'Yugoslavia in the 1970s: self-management and bargaining', *Journal of Comparative Economics*, 4, 2 (June), pp. 192–208.

Commons, John (1934), *Institutional Economics* (New York, NY: Macmillan).

Connor, James and Branko Vukmir (1976), 'The legal anatomy of a Yugoslav enterprise', *Business Lawyer*, 32, 1 (November), pp. 99–117.

Constitution of the Socialist Federal Republic of Yugoslavia, adopted 31 January 1974; published in book form in Ljublijana in 1974 by Dopisna Delavska Univerza.

Cook, Paul, Jr (1955), 'Decentralization and the transfer price problem', *Journal of Business*, 28, 2 (April), pp. 87–94.

Dahlman, Carl (1979), 'The problem of externality', *Journal of Law and Economics*, 22, 1 (April), pp. 141–62.

Dean, Joel (1955), 'Decentralization and intracompany pricing', *Harvard Business Review*, 33, 4 (July), pp. 65–74.

Dearden, John (1962), 'Mirage of profit decentralization'. *Harvard Business Review*, 40, 6 (November), pp. 140–54.

Doder, Dusko (1978), *The Yugoslavs* (New York, NY: Random House).

Domar, E. D. (1966), 'The Soviet collective farm as a producer cooperative', *American Economic Review*, 56, 4 (September), pp. 734–57.

Ekonomska Politika, published weekly in Belgrade.

Feinberg, Robert M. (1981), 'On the measurement of aggregate concentration', *Journal of Industrial Economics*, 30, 2 (December), pp. 217–22.

Feld, Werner J. (1982), 'Transfer pricing of multinational enterprises: toward a new code of conduct', in Wolfram F. Hanrieder (ed.), *Economic Issues and the Atlantic Community* (New York, NY: Praeger), pp. 115–38.

Furubotn, Eirik G. (1971), 'Towards a dynamic model of the Yugoslav firm', *Canadian Journal of Economics*, 4, 2 (May), pp. 182–97.

Furubotn, Eirik G. (1974), 'Bank credit and the labor-managed firm: the Yugoslav case', *Canadian–American Slavic Studies*; reprinted as chapter 18 in Furubotn and Pejovich (eds), *The Economics of Property Rights* (Cambridge, Mass.: Ballinger, 1974).

Furubotn, Eirik G. (1976), 'The long-run analysis of the labor-managed firm: an alternative interpretation', *American Economic Review*, 66, 1 (March), pp. 104–23.

Furubotn, Eirik G. (1980a), 'The socialist labor-managed firm and bank-financed investment: some theoretical issues', *Journal of Comparative Economics*, 4, 2 (June), pp. 184–91.
Furubotn, Eirik G. (1980b) 'Bank credit and the labor-managed firm: reply', *American Economic Review*, 70, 4 (September), pp. 800–4.
Furubotn, Eirik G. and Svetozar Pejovich (1970), 'Property rights and the behavior of the firm in a socialist state: the example of Yugoslavia', *Zeitschrift für Nationalökonomie*, 30, 3–4, pp. 431–54; reprinted as chapter 16 in Furubotn and Pejovich (eds), *The Economics of Property Rights* (Cambridge, Mass.: Ballinger, 1974).
Furubotn, Eirik G. and Svetozar Pejovich (1973), 'Property rights, economic decentralization and the evolution of the Yugoslav firm, 1965–72', *Journal of Law and Economics*, 16, 2 (October), pp. 275–302.
Furubotn, Eirik G. and Svetozar Pejovich (1974), *The Economics of Property Rights* (Cambridge, Mass.: Ballinger).
Galbraith, John Kenneth (1967), 'Review of a review', *The Public Interest*, 9 (Fall), pp. 109–18.
Gorlin, Alice (1974), 'Socialist corporations: the wave of the future in the USSR?' in Morris Bornstein and Daniel Fusfeld (eds), *The Soviet Economy* (Homewood, Ill.: Irwin).
Gorlin, Alice (1976a), 'Industrial reorganization: the associations', in *Soviet Economy in a New Perspective* (Washington, DC: US Congress Joint Economic Committee 14 October), pp. 162–88.
Gorlin, Alice (1976b), 'Management of Soviet associations', *The ACES Bulletin*, 18, 1 (Spring), pp. 45–66.
Granick, David (1975a), *Enterprise Guidance in Eastern Europe* (Princeton, NJ: Princeton University Press).
Granick, David (1975b), 'National differences in the use of internal transfer prices', *California Management Review*, 17, 4 (Summer), pp. 28–40.
Green, Donald W. (1977), 'Associations and the post-command economy: executive Bolshevism in the Soviet Union', *Soviet Union*, 4, 2, pp. 330–43.
Hart, P. E. and S. J. Prais (1956), 'The analysis of business concentration: a statistical approach', *Journal of the Royal Statistical Society*, ser. A, 119, part 2, pp. 150–81.
Heflebower, Richard B. (1960), 'Observations on decentralization in large enterprises', *Journal of Industrial Economics*, 9, 1 (November), pp. 7–22.
Heinritz, Stuart, F. (1947), *Purchasing* (Englewood Cliffs, NJ: Prentice-Hall).
Hirshleifer, Jack (1956), 'On the economics of transfer pricing', *Journal of Business*, 29, 3 (July), pp. 172–84.
Hirshleifer, Jack (1957), 'Economics of the divisionalized firm', *Journal of Business*, 30, 2 (April), pp. 96–108.
Hohmann, H. H., M. Kaser and K. Thalheim (eds) (1975), *The New Economic Systems of Eastern Europe* (Berkeley, Calif.: University of California Press).
Holesovsky, Vaclav (1973), 'Planning and the market in the Czechoslovak reform', in Morris Bornstein (ed.), *Plan and Market* (New Haven, Conn.: Yale University Press).
Horvat, Branko (1976), *The Yugoslav Economic System: The First Labor-*

Managed Economy in the Making (White Plains, NY: International Arts and Sciences Press).

Hurwicz, Leonid (1973), 'The design of mechanisms for resource allocation', *American Economic Review*, 63, 2 (May), pp. 1–30.

Kaser, Michael and J. Zielinski (1970), *Planning in East Europe* (London: The Bodley Head).

Katz. Abraham (1972), *The Politics of Economic Reform in the Soviet Union* (New York, NY: Praeger).

Keren, Michael (1973), 'Concentration amid devolution in East Germany's reforms', in Morris Bornstein (ed.), *Plan and Market* (New Haven, Conn.: Yale University Press).

Kessler, Friedrich and Richard H. Stern (1959), 'Competition, contract, and vertical integration', *The Yale Law Journal*, 69, 1 (November), pp. 1–129.

Klein, Benjamin, Robert G. Crawford and Armen A. Alchian (1978), 'Vertical integration, appropriable rents, and the competitive contracting process', *Journal of Law and Economics*, 21, 2 (October), pp. 297–326.

Lavigne, Marie (1975), *The Socialist Economies of the Soviet Union and Europe* (White Plains, NY: International Arts and Sciences Press).

Law on Associated Labor (Zakon o Udruženom Radu), adopted 25 November 1976; published in book form in Belgrade in 1976 by Službeni List.

MacMillan, Keith and David Farmer (1979), 'Redefining the boundaries of the firm', *Journal of Industrial Economics*, 27, 3 (March), pp. 277–85.

Marczewski, Jan (1974), *Crisis in Socialist Planning* (New York, NY: Praeger).

Meade, James E. (1970), *The Theory of Indicative Planning* (Manchester: University of Manchester Press).

Meade, James E. (1971), *The Controlled Economy* (London: George Allen & Unwin).

Meade, James E. (1972), 'The theory of labour-managed firms and profit sharing', *Economic Journal*, 82, 1 (supplement) (March), pp. 402–28.

Meade, James E. (1974), 'Labour-managed firms in conditions of imperfect competition', *Economic Journal*, 84, 4 (December), pp. 817–24.

Milenkovitch, Deborah D. (1977), 'The case of Yugoslavia', *American Economic Review*, 67, 1 (Proc.) (February), pp. 55–60.

Milenkovitch, Deborah D. (1983), 'Is market socialism efficient?' in Andrew Zimbalist (ed.), *Comparative Economic Systems: An Assessment of Knowledge, Theory, and Method* (Boston, Mass.: Kluwej-Nijhoff).

Nova Makedonija, published weekly in Skopje.

Nuti, D. M. (1977), 'Large corporations and the reform of Polish industry', *Jahrbuch der Wirtschaft Osteuropas*, 7, pp. 345–405.

Pejovich, Svetozar (1973), 'The banking system and the investment behavior of the Yugoslav firm', in Morris Bornstein (ed.), *Plan and Market* (New Haven, Conn.: Yale University Press).

Politika, published daily in Belgrade.

Pryor, Frederic L. (1973), *Property and Industrial Organization in Communist and Capitalist Nations* (Bloomington, Ind.: Indiana University Press).

Roberts, Paul C. (1971), *Alienation and the Soviet Economy* (Albuquerque: University of New Mexico Press).

Rockwell, Charles S. (1968), 'An international comparison of the size and efficiency of the Yugoslav plant', Center Discussion Paper No. 47 (New Haven, Conn.: Yale University, Economic Growth Center, February).
Rugman, Alan M. (1979), *International Diversification and the Multinational Enterprise* (Lexington, Mass.: Heath).
Sacks, Stephen R. (1973), *Entry of New Competitors in Yugoslav Market Socialism* (Berkeley, Calif.: Institute of International Studies).
Sacks, Stephen R. (1977), 'Transfer prices in decentralized self-managed enterprises', *Journal of Comparative Economics*, 1, 2 (June), pp. 183–93.
Sacks, Stephen R. (1978), 'The private sector in Yugoslavia', *ACES Bulletin*, 20, 2 (Summer), pp. 1–11.
Sacks, Stephen R. (1980), 'Divisionalization in large Yugoslav enterprises', *Journal of Comparative Economics*, 4, 2 (June), pp. 209–25.
Sacks, Stephen R. (1982), 'Corporate giants in Yugoslavia', in Derek Jones and Jan Svejnar (eds), *Participatory and Self-Managed Firms* (Lexington, Mass.: D. C. Heath).
Savezni Zavod za Statistiku (SZS) [Federal Institute for Statistics], *Statistički Bilten* [Statistical Bulletin], No. 627 (August 1970) and No. 1274 (December 1981), both titled 'Industrija'.
Savezni Zavod za Statistiku [Federal Institute for Statistics], *Statistički Godišnjak Jugoslavije* [Statistical Yearbook of Yugoslavia], published annually in Belgrade.
Scherer, F. M. (1980), *Industrial Market Structure and Economic Performance*, 2nd edn. (Chicago: Rand McNally); 1st edn, 1970.
Schrenk, Martin, Cyrus Ardalan and Nawal El Tatawy (1979), *Yugoslavia: Self-Management Socialism and the Challenges of Development* (Baltimore, Md.: Johns Hopkins Press).
Schrenk, Martin (1981), 'Managerial structures and practices in manufacturing enterprises: a Yugoslav case study', *World Bank Staff Working Paper*, No. 455 (Washington, DC: The World Bank, May).
Schroeder, Gertrude E. (1979), 'The Soviet economy on a treadmill of "reforms" ', in *Soviet Economy in a Time of Change* (Washington, DC: US Congress Joint Economic Committee, 10 October).
Sirc, Ljubo (1979), *The Yugoslav Economy Under Self-Management* (New York, NY: St Martin's Press).
Smolinski, Leon (1974), 'Towards a socialist corporation: Soviet industrial reorganization of 1973', *Survey*, 20, 1 (Winter), pp. 24–35.
Solomons, David (1965), *Divisional Performance: Measurement and Control* (Homewood, Ill.: Irwin).
Spigler, Iancu (1973), *Economic Reform in Rumanian Industry* (London: Oxford University Press).
Steinherr, Alfred (1975), 'Profit-maximizing vs. labor-managed firms: a comparison of market structure and firm behavior', *Journal of Industrial Economics*, 24, 2 (December), pp. 97–104.
Steinherr, Alfred (1977), 'On the efficiency of profit sharing and labor participation in management', *Bell Journal of Economics*, 8, 2 (Autumn), pp. 545–55.

Steinherr, Alfred and Henk Peer (1975), 'Worker management and the modern industrial enterprise: a note', *Quarterly Journal of Economics*, 89, 4 (November), pp. 662–9.
Stephen, Frank H. (1978), 'Bank credit and investment by the Yugoslav firm', *Economic Analysis*, 12, 3 (Fall), pp. 221–40.
Stephen, Frank H. (1980), 'Bank credit and the labor-managed firm: comment', *American Economic Review*, 70, 4 (September), pp. 796–9.
Stigler, George J. (1951), 'The division of labor is limited by the extent of the market', *Journal of Political Economy*, 59, 3 (June), pp. 185–93.
Stigler, George J. (1958), 'The economics of scale', *Journal of Law and Economics*, 1 (October), pp. 54–71.
Triffin, Robert (1940), *Monopolistic Competition and General Equilibrium Theory* (Cambridge, Mass.: Harvard University Press).
Tyson, Laura D'Andrea (1979), 'Incentives, income sharing, and institutional innovation in the Yugoslav self-managed firm', *Journal of Comparative Economics*, 3, 3 (September), pp. 285–301.
Tyson, Laura D'Andrea (1980), *The Yugoslav Economic System and Its Performance in the 1970s* (Berkeley, Calif.: Institute of International Studies).
Vanek, Jaroslav (1970), *The General Theory of Labor-Managed Market Economies* (Ithaca, NY: Cornell University Press).
Vanek, Jaroslav (1971), 'The basic theory of financing of participatory firms', mimeo; reprinted as chapter 28 in Jaroslav Vanek (ed.), *Self-Management: Economic Liberation of Man* (Baltimore, MD.: Penguin, 1975).
Vanek, Jaroslav (1977), *The Labor-Managed Economy* (Ithaca, NY: Cornell University Press).
Vacić, Aleksandar M. (1978), 'The socio-economic content, the formation and distribution of income in a Yugoslav self-management economic unit (BOAL)', mimeo, presented at Dubrovnik (October).
Vacić, Aleksandar M. (1976), *Principi i Politika Dohotka* [Principles and Policies of Income] (Belgrade: Radnička Štampa).
Ward, Benjamin N. (1958), 'The firm in Illyria: market syndicalism', *American Economic Review*, 48, 4 (September), pp. 566–89; reprinted as chapter 8 in Ward *The Socialist Economy* (New York, NY: Random House, 1967).
Ward, Benjamin N. (1967), *The Socialist Economy: A Study of Organizational Alternatives* (New York, NY: Random House).
Whinston, Andrew (1964), 'Price guides in decentralized organizations', in W. W. Cooper *et al.* (eds), *New Perspectives in Organization Research* (New York, NY: John Wiley & Sons).
White, Lawrence J. (1981a), 'What has been happening to aggregate concentration in the United States', *Journal of Industrial Economics*, 29, 3 (March), pp. 223–30.
White, Lawrence J. (1981b), 'On measuring aggregate concentration: a reply', *Journal of Industrial Economics*, 30, 2 (December), pp. 223–4.
Williamson, Oliver E. (1970), *Corporate Control and Business Behavior* (Englewood Cliffs, NJ: Prentice-Hall).
Williamson, Oliver E. (1971), 'The vertical integration of production: market

failure considerations', *American Economic Review*, 61, 2 (May), pp. 112–23.

Williamson, Oliver E. (1975), *Markets and Hierarchies: Analysis and Antitrust Implications* (New York, NY: Free Press).

Williamson, Oliver E. (1979), 'Transaction-cost economics: the governance of contractual relations', *Journal of Law and Economics*, 22, 2 (October), pp. 233–62.

Woroniak, Alexander (1969), 'Industrial concentration in Eastern Europe: the search for optimum size and efficiency', in E. Salin and J. Stohler (eds), *Notwendigkeit und Gefahr der Wirtschaftlichen Konzentration* (Basle: Kyklos).

Zapp, Kenneth (1983), 'Self-management: lessons from the Yugoslav experience', manuscript.

Zielinski, J. G. (1973), *Economic Reforms in Polish Industry* (London: Oxford University Press).

Index

References in **bold** denote chapters that are wholly concerned with the subjects to which they refer.

adaptive, sequential decision-making 61, 69, 74, 101, 107, 112, 115, 122, 126, 147, 149
administrative services 4–5, 10, 11, 16, 49–52, 103–4, 123, 146
agreements *see* contracts; self-management agreements
allocation: of labor 7, 47–52, *Fig* 48 56, 116–17, 119–21, 123, 125, 146, 149; of resources 2, 7, 10, 13, 16, 18–19, 23, 25, 47–59, 70, 101, 116–17, 119–21, 125–6
amortization funds 112, 116, 119–20
arbitration procedure 71, 104
assets: collective (non-owned) 76, 77–83, 88; individual (owned) 77–83; of large enterprises 30–6, *Fig* 31, *Figs* 34–5, 38, *Table* 38, *Table* 40, 41, 133
associations, socialist industrial 56, **128–42**, 150
autonomy, divisional/subunit 1–13, 15, 18–20, 39, 44, 59–60, 65–6, 69, 73, 100, 121–3, 133–5, 138, 143, 146

banks 24–5, 43, 81, 84, 86, 88–90, 96, 110, 112, 114, 125, 134; internal 87–90, 98, 105
basic organization of associated labor (BOAL) 3, 7, *Fig* 14, 41, 45n, 103–4, 111, 114, 122–4
BIGZ (Beogradski Izdavačko-Grafički Zavod) 105–9, 119–20, 125
BOALs 3, 7, *Fig* 14 41, 45n, 103–4, 111, 114, 122–4

borrowed funds 76, 81, 84–6, 88–94, 97, 111–13, 126, 147; *see also* loans
bounded rationality 61–2, 65–6, 69–70, 74, 135–6, 141, 147
Bulgaria 130, 133–4
business fund 76, 95–6, 98, 148
buying and selling: between divisions 3, 10, 19, 32, 65–74, 103–4, 143, 149, *see also* transfer prices; outside divisions 3, 8, 10, 12, 19, 103–4, 110, 123, 144, 149

Canada *Table* 38
capital 12–13, 26, 32–3, *Table* 32, 116–17, 119, 126; access to 24–5, 43, 145; interdivisional capital flows 10, 12–15, 20, 74–5, 121, 124–5, 145, 147–8; maintenance requirement 76–7, 89–92, 97, 148
capitalism/capitalist firms 1, 11, 18, 22–7, 38–9, *Table* 38, 47, 52–6, 58–60, 65, 71, 76–7, 83–4, 87–92, 130, 136–7, 141, 145
central control 1, 18–19, 25–6, 58, 66, 71, 122, 135, 137–8, 140, 143, 146
central planning 23, 128–9, 132–8, 140–1, 150
central workers' council 71, 122, 124
COAL 17
collusion 6, 11, 17, 20, 26, 43–4, 122–3
communication 59, 62, 68, 129
competition 6, 17, 20, 22–5, 27, 41, 43–5, 53–4, 121–3, 145–6
complex organization of associated labor (COAL) 17

conflict *see* disputes
Constitution (1974) 2, 21n, 39, 73, 108, 120, 122, 143
constitutional amendments (1971) 2, 39, 143
contracts 2, 7, 15–16, 23, 61–74, 135; incomplete long-term 12, 66–70, 72, 74, 108, 112, 126, 136, 147, 149; *see also* self-management agreements
corporate savings 84–6, 94–6, 98, 125, 147
corporations, large 1–2, 17, **22–45**; case studies in **100–27**; international 36, 38–9, *Table* 38; *see also* enterprises
costs *see* transaction costs
Crvena Zastava (CZ) 87, 118–21, 125
Czechoslovakia 130, 133–4

decentralization 1, 7, 19, 47, 59, 122, 134; *see also* divisionalization; divisions
decision-making 7, 16, 44, 76, 122, 135, 137–9, 146; adaptive, sequential 61, 69, 74, 101, 107, 112, 115, 122, 126, 147, 149; centralized *see* central control; central planning; *see also* autonomy, divisional/sub-unit; divisionalization
depreciation 76, 90–2, 94–8, 120, 148
disputes 8, 70–1, 73, 114–15, 117–18
dividend maximization *see* profit maximization
divisionalization 1–21, 41, 46n, 56, 89, 95, **128–42**, 143–7, 150; efficiency of 58–74
divisions 1–21; autonomy of 1–13, 15, 18–20, 39, 44, 59–60, 65–6, 69, 73, 100, 121–3, 133–5, 138, 143, 146; interdivisional investment 10, 12–16, 20, 74–6, 84, 88–98 100, 103, 106–8; number/size of 5, *Tables* 40, 41–4, *Fig* 42, 45n, 130–1, 146; relationship among

2–8, 10–17, 19–20, 41, 43–5, 59, 65–74, 100–5, 143, 146–7
Dvadeset Prvi Maj (DPM) 118–21, 125

East Germany 130, 132–4
Eastern Europe 18, 128–42; *see also* individual countries
economies of scale in production 9, 24, 133
efficiency, economic 1–2, 7, 20, 43, 61, 135–6, 139; of enterprise/divisionalized structure 11, 20, **58–74**, 143, 145–7; of resource allocation 13, 16, 23–5, 47–9, 54–7; *see also* inefficiency
Ekonomska Politika 27–8, *Tables* 28–9, 30–9, 41–2, 44
employment 5, 30–4, *Fig* 31, *Figs* 34–5, 36, 38, *Tables* 37–8, *Table* 40, 41, *Fig* 42, 44
Energoinvest 3, 12, 14
enterprises (Preduzeće) 1–21, 39, 128; definition of 11, 16–17; size of 5–6, **22–45**; structure of 2–3, 11–20, 143–6; *see also* divisionalization; divisions
expansion/modernization 10, 12, 14, 106, 118–19, 148

Fortune '500' list 30, 36, *Table* 37
France 15, 38–9
Furubotn/Pejovich bias 76–83, 86–90, 147

General Motors (GM) 1, 18, 23, 25
Germany: East 130, 132–4; West *Table* 38
gigantism 22, 44
Great Britain *Table* 38, 39

horizontal mergers 133, 137, 139, 142n
Hungary 129–30, 132–4, 142n

IMR (Industrija Motora iz Rakovice) 108, 113–19, 125
IMT (Industrija Mašina i Traktora) 108, 113–19, 125

INA 123, 126
income distribution 7, 16, 20, 56, 66, 69, 72–3, 101, 103, 105, 110–12, 115–16, 119, 122–6, 144, 150
income sharing 9, 12, 17, 59, 101, 106–8, 110, 118–21, 123, 125–6, 149
incomplete long-term contracts 12, 66–70, 72, 74, 108, 112, 126, 136, 147, 149; *see also* self-management agreements
industrial associations 56, **128–42**, 150
industrial enterprises, size of 5, *Tables* 28–9, 30–4, *Fig* 31, *Table* 32, *Fig* 34, 36–41, *Table* 37, *Table* 40, *Fig* 42, 44, 45n, 130–1; international *Table* 38, 38–9
inefficiency 1–2, 7, 20, 43, 136, 146–7; of resource allocation 13, 16, 23–5, 47–9, 54–7; *see also* efficiency
inflation 68, 76, 81–3, 97–9, 109, 120, 125, 147
information 15–16, 18, 61–3, 70, 131, 136, 139, 144; impactedness 62–3, 137–8; *see also* bounded rationality
integration *see* mergers
intentions, misrepresentation of 62–3
internal banks 87–90, 98, 105
international firm size 36, 38–9, *Table* 38
investment 3, 10, 12–15, 17, 23, 66, 100, 126, 134–5, 139–41; interdivisional 10, 12–15, 20, 74–6, 84, 88–98; joint 14–16, 100, 103, 106–8, 110–13, 118–21, 125, 145, 150; self-financed 75, 77–9, 81–9, 93–4, 97, 111, 125, 147–8; theory of investment decisions 13, **75–99**, 147–8; *see also* borrowed funds; capital; loans
Ivica Lovinćic 123–5

Japan 38–9, *Table* 38
joint business councils 106–7, 110, 112, 114–15, 121, 126, 149

joint investment 14–16, 100, 103, 106–8, 110–13, 118–21, 125, 145, 150
joint services *see* administrative services

khozraschet status 134
KLEK 122, 124
Komora 100, 110, 112, 115, 127n
Križevci Trgovačno 124

labor 26–7, *Tables* 28–9, 30–4, *Fig* 31 *Figs* 34–5, 36, 38, *Tables* 37–8; allocation of 7, 47–52, *Fig* 48, 56, 116–17, 119–21, 123, 125, 146, 149; past 13, 116–17, 119, 126, 150
large firms/work units *see* size of firms/work units
Law on Associated Labor, 1976 (LAL) 2–5, 10, 13–14, 21n, 39, 88, 108, 143
laws, economic 2–5, 10, 12–14, 39, 43, 45n, 66, 68, 71–3, 76, 88, 95, 100, 108, 143
LEK 124–6
Litostroj 123–4, 126
loans 25, 107, 114, 125; interdivisional 10, 12–15, 20, 75–6, 84, 88–98, 125, 145, 148; time duration of 10, 13, 77, 80, 82–3, 87, 90–4, 96–8, 107, 120, 124–5, 148–9; *see also* borrowed funds; joint investment
long-term contracts, incomplete 12, 66–70, 72, 74, 108, 112, 126, 136, 147, 149; *see also* self-management agreements

Mali Makiš 109–13, 119, 120, 125
management, central 8, 18–19, 66, 132; *see also* central control; central planning
market mechanism 1, 15, 17, 20, 22–6, 43, 45, 58, 60–1, 63–6, 129, 135–6, 145, 147, 150
market prices 7–10, 12, 18, 20, 53–4, 103, 122, 125–6, 144, 149

market sharing 6, 11–12, 16–17, 20, 43, 45, 123, 146
Markets and Hierarchies: Analysis and Antitrust Implications (Williamson) 59
MATROZ (Fabrika Celuloze i Papira Matroz) 105–9, 119–20, 125
maximization of profit 47–51, 60, 70, 113, 149
mergers 44–5, 67, 69, 101, 106, 109, 115, 130–3, 135, 141; horizontal 133, 137, 139, 142n; vertical 17, 62–5, 70, 72, 131, 133, 139–40
misrepresentation of intentions 62–3
Mladinska Knjiga 123–5
modernization/expansion 10, 12, 14, 106, 118–19, 148
Mondragon, Spanish cooperatives at 77, 87
multidivisional structure 18, 136–9, 141–2, 150; *see also* divisionalization; divisions; enterprises

Nikola Tesla 124
non-labor inputs 47, 52–6, 59, 116–17, 119–21, 125

opportunism 61–5, 70–4, 101, 129, 135–8, 141, 147, 149
organization of associated labor (OAL) 17

past labor 13, 116–17, 119, 126, 150
Petar Drapsin (PD) 118–21, 125
planned economies 128–42
planning 4, 6–7, 15–17, 20, 23, 66, 73, 128; central 23, 128–9, 132–8, 140–1, 150; polycentric 6, 20; *see also* self-management agreements
Poland 130, 132–4
political considerations 6, 10, 12, 25, 43, 58
polycentric planning 6, 20
post-contractual opportunistic behavior 64–5, 71–2
preduzeće – see enterprises

price fixing 17, 20, 45, 123, 146
prices 6–7, 11, 23–5, 43, 82, 111; market 7–10, 12, 18, 20, 53–4, 103, 122, 125–6, 144, 149; transfer 1–3, 6–12, 14–15, 19–20, 66–7, 72–3, 96, 101, 103, 115–17, 122–3, 125–6, 144–6, 149
Principi i Politika Dohotka (A. M. Vacić) 100
production association 131
production decisions 7, 15, 20, 25–6, 125–6, 149
profit 26–7, 75, 106, 125, 134; maximization 47–51, 60, 70, 113, 149; sharing 5, 9, 12–14, 24, 27, 58, 72–3, 89

quasi-rent 64–5

radna organizacija – see work organization
reinvestment, enterprise *see* self-financed investment
repayment period on loans 10, 13, 77, 80, 82–3, 87, 90–4, 96–8, 107, 120, 124–5, 148–9
research institutes 131–2
resource allocation 2, 7, 10, 13, 16, 18–20, 23, 25, 47–57, 70, 101, 125–6, 138–9, 146, 149; labor 7, 47–52, *Fig* 48, 56, 116–17, 119–21, 123, 125, 146, 149; non-labor 47, 52–6, 59, 116–17, 119–21, 125
risk sharing 12–14, 23, 88, 98, 123, 126, 150
Romania 130, 133–4

sales of large enterprises 30–6, *Fig* 31, *Figs* 34–5, 38, *Table* 38, 41
savings 77–84, 147–8; corporate 84–6, 94–6, 98, 125, 147
science-production association 131
self-financed investment 75, 77–9, 81–9, 93–4, 97, 111, 125, 147–8
self-management agreements 15–16, 20, 23, 66–70, 73; case studies **100–27**

selling, buying and *see* buying and selling
services, internal sale of *see* administrative services
sharing clauses 74, 101, 108, 112, 115, 122, 126, 147
size of firms/work units 5, 22, 26, 128–31, 145–6, 150; international 36, 38–9, *Table* 38; large 1–2, 5–6, 17, **22–45**, 143, 145–6; small 1, 19, 25–6, 33, 39, 41, 58, 129, 143, 145–6
small-numbers exchange environment 62–3, 72
solidarity, enterprise 10, 12, 20, 59, 66, 69–70, 122, 124, 144–5, 147
Soviet Union 1, 18, 26, 128–39, 142
Spanish cooperatives (Mondragon) 77, 87
specialization 6, 12, 109, 133
Statistical Institute 17, 39–41, 44, 45n
Statistical Yearbook of Yugoslavia 39, *Tables* 40, 41
Sweden *Table* 38

team production 63, 69
technology 33, 132, 141
trade sector enterprises, size of 5, *Tables* 28–9, 30–2, *Fig* 31, 35–6, *Fig* 35, *Table* 40, 41, *Fig* 42, 44, 45n, 131
transaction costs 10–11, 43, 60–2, 65–7, 73–4, 130, 135–6, 139–41, 147, 150

transfer prices 1–3, 6–12, 14–15, 19–20, 66–7, 72–3, 96, 101, 103, 115–17, 122–3, 125–6, 144–6, 149; theory of **47–57**
Tvornica Duhan Zagreb 122

uncertainty 10, 61, 97, 139–40, 144
United States of America 1, 6, 18–19, *Table* 38, 77, 142, 146–7

Vanek, J 22, 26–7, 43–4, 52, 56, 57n, 87, 92, 145–6
Varteks (Varaždinski Tekstilni Kombinat) 101–5, 125

wages 19–20, 81, 84, 94–5; *see also* income distribution; income sharing
West Germany *Table* 38
Western Europe 18, 134, 142, 150; *see also* individual countries
Williamson, Oliver 18, 59–63, 65–6, 69–70, 72–3, 135–41, 147; *Markets and Hierarchies: Analysis and Antitrust Implications* 59
Winchester Repeating Arms Co. 60
work communities 4–5, 6, 10, 123–4
work organizations (*radna organizacija*) 17, 39, 45n, 103–4
work units, size of *see* size of firms/work units
workers, numbers of *see* employment

Zapp cases 122–4